# Medieval
# SIMULATIONS

## Challenging

*Written by Max W. Fischer*

**Teacher Created Materials, Inc.**
6421 Industry Way
Westminster, CA 92683
www.teachercreated.com

©2000 Teacher Created Materials, Inc.
Made in U.S.A.

**ISBN 1-57690-583-7**

*Edited by*
*Lorin Klistoff, M.A.*

*Illustrated by*
*Howard Chaney*

*Cover Art by*
*Cheri Macoubrie Wilson*

# Table of Contents

# Introduction

Anyone who has spent much time at all as a middle school educator has heard the perpetual lament of this specific group of students, "Why do we have to learn this?" Motivation is the key to this age level. *Medieval Simulations* has been designed to establish relevance between the distant past and the students' present existence.

This resource is predicated upon the concept that while cultures and circumstances may change over the centuries, basic human nature is a constant which binds us together. *Medieval Simulations* places students in meaningful classroom learning situations that replicate circumstances of significant events and/or cultures in the era between the fall of Rome and the Renaissance.

Through the use of problem-solving scenarios, classroom simulations, and simulated review games, the 23 activities within *Medieval Simulations* have been designed to merge higher-level thinking skills with an affective learning approach. It is a valuable instructional tool that promotes critical thinking among students.

*Medieval Simulations* allows the students of today to actively reflect upon the struggles and ambitions of peoples from one thousand years ago and compare them to the frustrations and aspirations of the world today.

Simulations of the type that appear in this collection bring to life the problems that challenged the peoples of yesterday, that trouble the peoples of today, and perhaps will prefigure solutions for the peoples of tomorrow. In these simulations, students engage in the great adventure of life—an adventure spanning the centuries, crossing ethnicity and region, and binding us all to membership in the human race.

**Note:** Although the activities in this book are simulations designed to reflect the events and conditions of the past, they should be handled with sensitivity and an awareness of the academic, social, and emotional atmosphere in the classroom. As with any new activity, preview each simulation before attempting it in the classroom. Adapt the simulations to best suit your classroom needs.

# Success with Simulations

The activities in *Medieval Simulations* have been selected in order to get students involved with the history of medieval times by actually simulating conditions of a particular historical era within the limited confines of the school environment.

Whether you intend to use a simulation for the purposes of introduction, review, or as part of the closure process, it is good to establish procedures throughout each unit that will maintain consistency and organization. Suggestions on how to best utilize and store the units in this book follow.

## Simulation Format

Each simulation begins with a lesson plan designed to assist the teacher with the preparations and procedures necessary and closes with valuable background information which connects the simulation to the historical events being studied. The lesson plan for each simulation follows this format:

> - **Title of Simulation**
> - **Topic**
> - **Objective(s)**
> - **Materials**
> - **Preparation**
> - **Procedure**
> - **Background**
> - **For Discussion** (where applicable)
> - **Extension** (where applicable)

## Storing Simulations

As you use each activity, you will want to save the components of the simulation by using a readily available and well-organized system which will serve the future as well as the present. Labeled file folders or large manila envelopes can be easily sorted and organized by simulation units and kept in a file box. Pages that will be duplicated or made into overhead transparencies can be easily stored in the file folders or envelopes. Game cards, labels, etc., should be placed in envelopes or resealable plastic bags before storing them in their respective folders. If possible, use index paper or card stock for reproduced items, such as game pieces, that will be reused. Laminating will help preserve these items.

Outside materials, such as candy or plastic spoons, should be readily available and noted on the outside of the activity folder to serve as a reminder that these items need to be accessible for the simulation.

Once the simulations have been organized into a file box, you will be prepared for each unit on a moment's notice.

Let the simulations begin!

# Cooperative Learning

Cooperative learning is an important instructional strategy because it can be used as an integral part of many educational processes. It is made to order for thinking activities. The cooperative learning process acts as a powerful motivational tool.

Many of the activities in this unit involve the cooperative learning process in a team effort to find solutions or come to conclusions regarding the simulations. With this in mind, consider the following information as you initiate team activities.

## The Four Basic Components of Cooperative Learning

1. **In cooperative learning, all group members need to work together to accomplish the task.** No one is finished until the whole group is finished and/or has come to consensus. The task or activity needs to be designed so that members are not just completing their own parts but are working to complete one product together.

2. **Cooperative learning groups should be heterogeneous.** It is helpful to start by organizing groups so that there is a balance of abilities within and among groups. Some of the simulations in this book, however, require a specific type of grouping for cooperative teams in order to achieve the simulation objective. Under such circumstances, a balanced, heterogeneous, cooperative learning team arrangement will not be appropriate for the success of the simulation.

3. **Cooperative learning activities need to be designed not only so that each student contributes to the group but also so that individual group members can be assessed on his or her performances.** This can be accomplished by assigning each member a role that is essential to the completion of the task or activity. When input must be gathered from all members of the group, no one can go along for a free ride.

4. **Cooperative learning teams need to know the social as well as the academic objectives of a lesson.** Students need to know what they are expected to learn and how they are supposed to be working together to accomplish the learning. Students need to process or think and talk about how they worked on social skills, as well as to evaluate how well their group worked on accomplishing the academic objective. Social skills are not something that students automatically know; these skills need to be taught.

# Sylvester Eimwright

## Topic

Early Christianity: first century (A.D.) Rome

## Objectives

1. Students will identify how their religious rights are protected.

2. Students will relate their feelings about religious intolerance.

## Materials

- one copy of the accompanying text, Elect Eimwright! (page 8)

- access to reference resources, such as encyclopedias

## Preparation

Make the required number of copies of the student text, Elect Eimwright!

## Procedure

1. Have students grouped in cooperative learning teams of two to four students per team.

2. Distribute the dilemma Elect Eimwright! (pronounced "I-am-right") and have students read it and answer its questions within their team, with one student serving as a recorder for the team's answers.

3. Time permitting, recorders from different teams may switch positions and share their responses with another team before whole class discussion begins. (This step is optional.)

4. The instructor should entertain a whole class discussion to bring the lesson to closure by having various teams share their answers to the dilemma's questions. (See page 7 for suggested answers.)

5. If the activity is to be used as an anticipatory set, the instructor should ask:

   - "What major modern religion started out being persecuted and picked upon like the people whose beliefs didn't agree with Sylvester Eimwright's?" *(Christianity)*

   - "What culture ruled over the earliest Christians and made their lives difficult?" *(the Romans)*

6

# Sylvester Eimwright *(cont.)*

## Procedure *(cont.)*

6. If the activity closes an introductory lesson about early Christianity that has already introduced Roman persecution of Christians, the teacher may ask:

   • "In what major ways did Christian beliefs differ from those of Rome?" *(Christians refused to worship anyone, including the emperor, as a god except for God. Christians refused to join the army or government and criticized Roman religious festivals. They promoted Jesus' idea that all people would be equal in heaven.)*

   • "How did Christians suffer under Roman rule?" *(Christians were blamed for numerous tragedies, such as famines, plagues, and even the great fire of Rome in 64 A.D. Their religion was made illegal, and many Christians suffered death in Colosseum spectacles at the hands of wild animals and gladiators.)*

## Background

Following the Jewish practice of worshipping one god, the early Christian church of Rome put itself at odds with the empire by offering no idolatry to the Roman emperor. For the first several hundred years of the religion, poor farmers, workers, and slaves were its major converts as they eagerly sought the promise of a better life in the hereafter. As late as 300 A.D., the emperor Diocletian announced his "divine right" as emperor, declaring his right to rule came directly from the Roman gods. However, to demonstrate how deeply Christianity had worked itself into the fabric of Roman life (even upper-class life), by 313 A.D., the emperor Constantine legalized Christianity. Within that century, it became the official religion of the Roman Empire.

## Extension

Allow interested students to research the following questions for extra credit or as the nucleus for research projects:

   • Why did the framers of the U.S. Constitution specifically say the government could not establish a state church and people could have freedom of religion?

   • What present-day governments have harsh laws about obeying their country's religion?

---

### Answers to the discussion questions on page 8

1. Unemployment, depressed economic conditions, and weather-related disasters have hindered food production.

2. Answers will vary.

3. The First Amendment allows for freedom of religion while prohibiting the establishment of a state religion.

---

# Elect Eimwright!

The United States is suffering through another depression similar to the one of the 1930s. Many people are without jobs, and bad weather in the nation's West, Midwest, and South has hurt the production of crops. The United States is actually having to import food from other more fortunate nations.

Sylvester Eimwright (pronounced "I-am-right") promotes the idea that the problems the United States is facing stem from people not knowing the true god, his god. In fact, he has all the answers in a book given to him by an angel. People not believing in his god have led Americans to social and economic disaster. He has persuaded so many people to his way of thinking that he is running for president of the United States.

If elected, Mr. Eimwright pledges to make his religion the official state religion of the United States. Those not worshipping his way will lose their jobs and may be imprisoned. Others may be deported to their parents' original country (even though they are American citizens). Jobs will be for true believers only!

Public opinion polls show him to be a leading candidate for president.

## Questions to Consider

1. What problems face the United States as Mr. Eimwright is running for president?

   _____

   _____

   _____

2. Would you vote for Mr. Eimwright? Why or why not?

   _____

   _____

   _____

3. What part of the United States Constitution would Mr. Eimwright be violating if indeed he became president and tried to enact these new laws?

   _____

   _____

   _____

# Our Minister, the President?

## Topic

Early Christianity: Introduction into the Roman Empire by Constantine

## Objectives

1. Students will identify the circumstances of Christianity's acceptance by the Roman Empire.

2. Students will present a rationale why our government should or should not align itself with any particular religion.

## Materials

- one copy per student of the accompanying fallacious newspaper story Government to Promote Religion? (page 11) and Questions to Consider (page 12)

## Preparation

Make sufficient copies of the newspaper text and the accompanying questions.

## Procedure

1. After students have been presented information about the induction of Christianity as the official religion of the Roman Empire, place students in cooperative learning teams of three or four.

2. Distribute copies of the newspaper story and have students read through it, answering the accompanying questions within their teams. A team recorder could write down a team response to each question, or individuals could record their own responses. However, a team spokesperson should be assigned to present the views of the group to the rest of the class after a stipulated amount of time.

3. Have a team spokesperson present a summary of views on each question to the entire class. It is not necessary to have each team respond to each question in whole class sharing, especially if time is limited. (See page 10 for suggested answers.)

4. Ask the class the following questions:

- "Do you think this article is an actual account of the president's wishes? Why or why not?"

- "What part of our country's laws would stop any leader or lawmaker(s) from forcing a particular religion onto the people?" *(First Amendment—freedom of religion; Congress shall not establish a law respecting an establishment of religion.)*

- "If parents want their children to have an education with a religious character to it, what options do they have?" *(They may enroll their children in nearby parochial schools for the cost of tuition.)*

# Our Minister, the President? *(cont.)*

## Background

After a legendary victory in battle in 312 A.D. in which he supposedly received a vision from God about his triumph, the emperor Constantine untied the Roman knot that had stifled Christianity for three hundred years. In his Edict of Milan, he gave all of Rome's subjects religious freedom and legalized Christianity. Furthermore, he used state tax funds to build Christian churches and schools. He allowed church officials to join government service and escape the payment of taxes. This was quite a turnabout for an empire that as recently as the previous emperor had officially espoused the idea that the emperor received his orders to rule from the Roman gods!

By the end of the fourth century, the emperor Theodosius went one step further. He made Christianity the official religion of the empire and outlawed every other religion.

## Extension

- A possible essay question that students could respond to would be, "Should public schools promote one religion over any others? Why or why not?"

- Some interested students may wish to research whether their city or state has a voucher plan to give tax dollars to parents who enroll their children in private (including parochial) schools.

---

### Answers for questions on page 12

1. Answers will vary.

2. Answers will vary. Be prepared for some variations in students' responses. While many, even most, students would oppose such presidential action, some may favor it. Students should be encouraged to state reasonable logic for their positions.

3. Similarities would include the attempt to make an official state religion, use tax money to build religious schools, outlaw other religions, and have church leaders as government officials.

---

# Government to Promote Religion?

*by Lars Schilmin*
*Washington, D.C.*

Reports out of Washington yesterday seem to confirm what many concerned Americans have wondered aloud over the past several months. The president is apparently ready to announce a plan whereby government tax money will be used to build new religious schools that will promote his church affiliation. Furthermore, the same reports indicate that the president is ready to replace several key (yet unnamed) cabinet members with various leaders of his church.

Unnamed senators have expressed displeasure with the president's plan, which he is set to announce at a news conference next week.

Since the president's impeachment acquittal last year, stories have surfaced about his newfound love of his church. He has claimed his religion and has saved his presidency.

"The president has seen a new light."

A close escape from death in a car accident several months ago cemented the president's determination to pursue this plan.

Another portion of his plan is to outlaw certain religions with which his church disagrees. Upon further questioning, a White House spokesman would only say, "The president has seen a new light."

# Government to Promote Religion? *(cont.)*

## *Questions to Consider*

**Directions:** Read the article on page 11 and answer the questions.

1. Should tax money from the government go to fund religious schools? Why or why not?

_____

_____

_____

_____

_____

_____

_____

2. Would you support such an action by our president or government?

_____

_____

_____

_____

_____

_____

_____

3. How is this similar to the beginnings of the Christian church under Constantine and Theodosius in the Roman Empire?

_____

_____

_____

_____

_____

_____

# Ordeal for Truth

## Topic

Germanic Barbarians:  their justice system

## Objective

Students will identify three ways Germanic barbarians of the early Middle Ages set about to determine the truth in criminal and civil cases.

## Materials

- a set of true/false questions that pertain to a section of text students are reading concerning barbarians of medieval Europe

## Preparation

Create a work sheet with a set of true/false questions that deal with a specific section of text that students have not yet read and make sufficient copies so that each student has one.

## Procedure

1. Before students have read a specific section of text on barbarian life in the early Middle Ages, have them take educated "guesses" on the true/false work sheet you have given them.

2. After a few minutes, survey the class on each item as to how many students thought an item was true or false.  Then instruct students to read the specific segment of text.

3. After students have read the text (or while they are reading it), they are to verify the various answers for the true or false questions.

4. After students have had sufficient time to complete the reading and correct answers on the work sheet, the barbarian-like ordeals will begin to determine the accuracy and truth of student responses.  (See Extension.)  For these classroom ordeals, prompt the class with background information on how Germanic barbarians of the fifth through tenth centuries sought to determine the truth in criminal and civil cases, especially if witnesses were lacking.  Pick willing students and always use a teacher's good common sense.  Make sure the ordeal is more comical than embarrassing and never threatening or dangerous!

5. Select one of the work sheet's true or false questions and a student volunteer.  Select and explain a particular classroom ordeal.  (See Extension.)  The student is to give his or her response to the particular true or false question.  Then he or she proceeds with the ordeal.  Supposedly, if the ordeal is successfully completed, his or her answer is presumed correct.

# Ordeal for Truth *(cont.)*

## *Procedure* *(cont.)*

6. The rest of the class may confirm or dispute the actual answer in light of a successful ordeal. This may also be the basis of discussing how accurate such tasks were in determining truth in Europe fifteen hundred years ago.

## *Background*

The Germanic barbarians of Central Europe during the early Middle Ages had several methods for determining truth when injustices had occurred. One method had accused parties swear to their own innocence along with the sworn oaths of corroborating witnesses to attest to the accused's innocence. They believed anyone who would swear by the gods would be punished if they had lied.

When there were no witnesses available to side with an accused person, that individual would have to undergo an ordeal. These physical trials were fraught with pain and the possibility of death. However, to prove one's innocence, they would be necessary. The accused would put his arm (up to the elbow) into a boiling pot of water to withdraw a stone. The wound would be bandaged, and after three days if the arm had healed, the accused was released. If the skin had become scalded, he would be found guilty. In a similar way, another ordeal had a defendant walk over red-hot coals or hold a heated iron in his hands. Again, the wound would be bandaged for three days before the fate of the defendant was determined. A third ordeal had the accused thrown into a river or lake while being tied to a pole on shore. If the suspect sank to the bottom, his innocence was proven (provided he could be hauled to the surface before he had drowned). A floating defendant was a guilty defendant.

The latter method was still in use during the early colonial era of America as a test for witches. The hot iron ordeal goes back in history as far as Hammurabi's Code (1792 B.C.), and it is still used today by some desert Bedouin tribesmen in North Africa and the Middle East to ensure justice.

The true or false questions serve as more than just a prompt for this simulation. True or false questions given prior to any text-based reading serve as a comprehension prompt. The subject of each question alerts readers to critical topics within the reading.

# Ordeal for Truth *(cont.)*

## *Extension*

Possible classroom "ordeals" might include the following:

- Hold a textbook in each outstretched hand for one minute.

- Stand at attention in the front of the room without blinking for one minute.

- Balance a book on top of one's head for a prescribed period of time or walk backwards a set distance with the book balanced on the head. (The book must not fall.) Make sure the way is cleared of any obstructions.

- Vertically balance a pencil on the tip of one's index finger for 30 seconds.

- Given some bubble gum, blow a bubble the size of a softball.

Obviously, there are numerous other possibilities. Remember, keep any "ordeal" safe, fun, and gentle in spirit.

# Barbarian Jeopardy

## Topic

Barbarians of Early Middle Ages:  European geography

## Objectives

1. Students will identify six barbarian tribes of Western Europe during the early Middle Ages.

2. They will utilize geographic skills, such as latitude/longitude and map scale, to compare locations of barbarian kingdoms within the land areas of modern European nations.

## Materials

- accompanying Barbarian Territories (about 500 A.D.) map (page 21)

- an overhead projector and transparency sheet

- accompanying set of questions for Barbarian Jeopardy (pages 19 and 20), or a similar set created by the classroom instructor

- current maps of Europe (Those found in the back of recent social studies textbooks that show latitude and longitude lines are acceptable.)

- accompanying Jeopardy question game board sheet (page 18)

- ruler for each student

## Preparation

1. Make one copy of the map, Barbarian Territories (about 500 A.D.), for every two students.

2. Make an overhead transparency of the aforementioned map and the Jeopardy board.

3. Make sure each student team of two has a current map of Europe to use for reference.

4. If the teacher is not using the supplied questions for Barbarian Jeopardy, a sufficient number of questions needs to be created by the teacher.

## Procedure

1. Have students in cooperative teams of four pupils work as "sharing pairs," two pairs of students with each pair sharing a recent map of Europe and the outline map "Barbarian Territories."

2. Teams take turns selecting a topic and a question with a specific point value.  The team whose turn it is will have one minute to answer the question.  (Unlike the real Jeopardy game show, answers need not be in question form.)  If they are correct, that team earns the points.  However, if the team is incorrect, the first team to raise their hands with the correct answer and be recognized by the teacher will take the points.

# Barbarian Jeopardy *(cont.)*

## Procedure *(cont.)*

3. As each point value is used up in a category, it should be marked out on the transparency by the teacher.

4. The game continues on a rotational basis until all questions are used or time runs out.

## Background

Nomadic herders from Northern Europe, ancestors of the later Vikings, resisted Roman authority and eventually overtook it. From the fifth through tenth centuries, they controlled large sections of Western Europe through numerous small bands and their chieftains.

These tribes included the Vandals, Saxons, Angles, Franks, Goths, Visigoths, and Ostrogoths. Most spoke Germanic dialects and are often referred to as Germanic barbarians. As they were assimilated by the very cultures whose people they defeated, some of these barbarians became the foundation of the future nations of England, Germany (Angles and Saxons), and France (Franks).

By having students work in pairs within teams, an optimum learning environment is stimulated where greater involvement is attained and, hopefully, more learning occurs. Pairs should work on the question with the geographic skill required within the first 30 seconds; take some time to share; and if necessary, use the latter fifteen seconds to rework the item before giving a final answer.

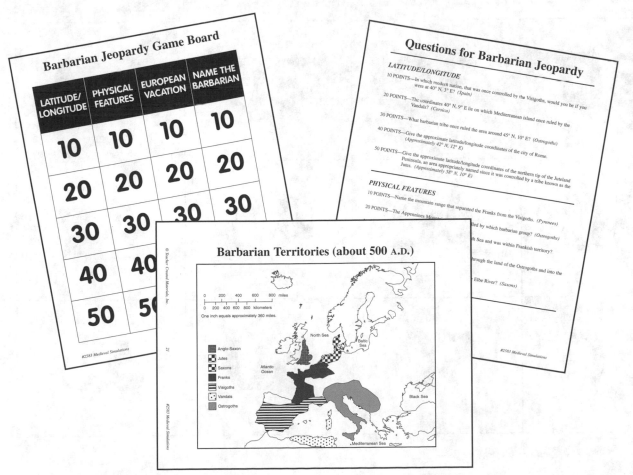

# Barbarian Jeopardy Game Board

| LATITUDE/ LONGITUDE | PHYSICAL FEATURES | EUROPEAN VACATION | NAME THE BARBARIAN |
|---|---|---|---|
| 10 | 10 | 10 | 10 |
| 20 | 20 | 20 | 20 |
| 30 | 30 | 30 | 30 |
| 40 | 40 | 40 | 40 |
| 50 | 50 | 50 | 50 |

# Questions for Barbarian Jeopardy

## LATITUDE/LONGITUDE

10 POINTS—In which modern nation, that was once controlled by the Visigoths, would you be if you were at 40° N, 3° E? *(Spain)*

20 POINTS—The coordinates 42° N, 9° E lie on which Mediterranean island once ruled by the Vandals? *(Corsica)*

30 POINTS—What barbarian tribe once ruled the area around 45° N, 10° E? *(Ostrogoths)*

40 POINTS—Give the approximate latitude/longitude coordinates of the city of Rome. *(Approximately 42° N, 12° E)*

50 POINTS—Give the approximate latitude/longitude coordinates of the northern tip of the Juteland Peninsula, an area appropriately named since it was controlled by a tribe known as the Jutes. *(Approximately 58° N, 10° E)*

## PHYSICAL FEATURES

10 POINTS—Name the mountain range that separated the Franks from the Visigoths. *(Pyrenees)*

20 POINTS—The Appennines Mountains were controlled by which barbarian group? *(Ostrogoths)*

30 POINTS—Which major river flows northward into the North Sea and was within Frankish territory? *(Rhine River)*

40 POINTS—Which river flows eastward from the Alps through the land of the Ostrogoths and into the Black Sea? *(Danube River)*

50 POINTS—Which barbarian kingdom stretched along the Elbe River? *(Saxons)*

# Questions for Barbarian Jeopardy *(cont.)*

## EUROPEAN VACATION

10 POINTS—Which modern European nation was named after the Franks? *(France)*

20 POINTS—The area of which two nations on the Iberian Peninsula was once controlled by the Visigoths? *(Spain and Portugal)*

30 POINTS—Name the modern European nation found on the Juteland Peninsula. *(Denmark)*

40 POINTS—The land area of which modern nation in Central Europe was not controlled by a barbarian tribe according to the map? *(Switzerland)*

50 POINTS—Island parts of which two modern European nations were controlled by the Vandals in 500 A.D.? *(France and Italy)*

## NAME THE BARBARIAN

Given the names of three modern nations, name the barbarian tribe that controlled that land area in 500 A.D.

10 POINTS—Italy, Austria, Slovenia *(Ostrogoths)*

20 POINTS—France, Belgium, Germany *(Franks)*

30 POINTS—Andorra, France, Monaco *(Visigoths)*

40 POINTS—Netherlands, Germany, Denmark *(Saxons)*

50 POINTS—France, Italy, Tunisia (North Africa) *(Vandals)*

# Barbarian Territories (about 500 A.D.)

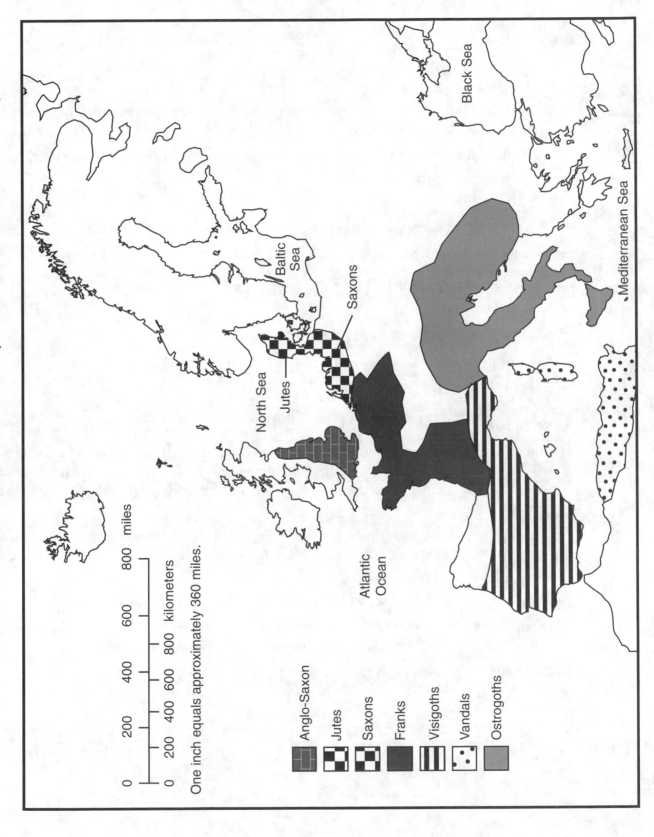

Black Sea

Mediterranean Sea

Baltic Sea

Saxons

North Sea

Jutes

Atlantic Ocean

800 miles

| 0 | 200 | 400 | 600 | 800 | miles |

| 0 | 200 | 400 | 600 | 800 | kilometers |

One inch equals approximately 360 miles.

Anglo-Saxon

Jutes

Saxons

Franks

Visigoths

Vandals

Ostrogoths

# Barbarian Navigator

## Topic

Barbarian Migrations

## Objectives

1. Students will use a map detailing migratory routes of European barbarian tribes to solve problems employing map scale.

2. Students will identify the general origins and destinations of several barbarian tribes.

## Materials

- the accompanying map, Barbarian Migration (100–500 A.D.) on page 27
- the accompanying Barbarian Name Tags (page 26)
- the accompanying Barbarian Hardship Cards (page 25)
- several dice
- one two-inch (5-cm) white twist tie for each pair of students
- maps of modern Europe, either in a text or an atlas
- ruler for each student

## Preparation

1. This activity is designed to promote cooperative learning, and so it would be ideal to have one copy of the map, Barbarian Migration (100–500 A.D.), for each pair of students in the class. However, some teachers may deem it better for each student to have his or her own copy.

2. Copy and cut out enough Barbarian Name Tags so each student group of four will have one with which to identify themselves. Laminate these name cards for extended use in the future.

3. Copy and cut out the Barbarian Hardship Cards. Laminate them, as well, for future use.

4. On the blackboard or overhead, the teacher should list the following modern European nations: Romania, Greece, Croatia, Hungary, Spain, France, and Italy.

5. Obtain the dice, rulers, and twist ties.

# Barbarian Navigator *(cont.)*

## *Procedure*

1. Students are to be in cooperative groups of four, which will be split into pairs.

2. Randomly distribute a Barbarian Name Tag to each team of four students.

3. Student teams are to select one of the modern European nations listed on the board as a destination for their particular tribe of barbarians. Here are a few ground rules:

   • Students may select only a nation listed that is on the migratory route of their tribe as shown on the map. They will have to use contemporary maps of Europe in their text or an atlas to verify this.

   • Only the Huns may use the first eligible nation available on their route. All other tribes need to select at least the second available nation on their route. (e.g., For the Ostrogoths' migration, Romania is the first nation on the list that students would cross. They may not choose Romania. However, other prescribed nations on that migratory route—Hungary or Italy—could be selected as a final destination.)

4. Using the white twist ties, rulers, and the map scale, student teams will attempt to be the first team to advance to their final destination. As the map scale indicates, one inch represents 400 miles. Therefore, if the students mark their twist ties at quarter-inch intervals, each mark will represent 100 miles. (*Note:* Twist ties are used in order to negotiate the various curves encountered in measuring actual distance on such a specialty map. They are superior over string in holding their shape, and they can be more easily marked.)

5. On a rotational basis, each team will roll a die (or have the teacher do so, if only one is available). Any number except a **1** will represent hundreds of miles of travel on the tribe's migratory route. (e.g., If a **5** is rolled, that team may advance 500 miles (8 km), or an inch and a quarter, on their route towards their final destination.)

6. Rolling a **1** means that students will undoubtedly miss a turn as they are forced into selecting a Barbarian Hardship Card.

7. The first team to arrive at their destination is the winner.

# Barbarian Navigator *(cont.)*

## Background

Barbarian Navigator combines modern geography with the historical migration of European tribes in the latter days of the Roman Empire and early Middle Ages. Some tribes, such as the Franks, took the relatively short timespan of a century to traverse the Rhine from Germany into France. Those peoples listed on this activity's map meandered for several centuries, crisscrossing much of the continent. The Vandals even ended up settling in North Africa.

In working on the activity, teachers are encouraged to have students work in pairs as an optimum method for obtaining maximum student involvement and understanding. One map for four students could probably encourage the practice of one student in the group doing all the calculations. One map for each student might simply promote a sense of futility among lower ability students. While there are no guarantees, splitting foursomes into pairs usually increases involvement and limits frustration. Having pairs check each others' work (while other teams are taking their turn rolling the die) further promotes learning.

## Extension

Students may be prompted to do additional research on the following related topics:

- The fall of Rome, 476 A.D.

- How did each tribe get its name?

- Why was Attila the Hun known as "the Scourge of God"?

- Why did we get the words *vandal* and *vandalize* from the tribe of the same name?

# Barbarian Hardship Cards

TRAVEL DELAYED BY FLOODED RIVER. LOSE A TURN.

DISEASE STALKS THE TRIBE. ILLNESS DELAYS PROGRESS. LOSE A TURN.

EXTREME WINTER. BLIZZARD HALTS ALL TRAVEL. LOSE A TURN.

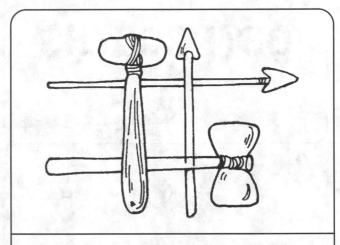

FIGHTING WITH OTHER TRIBES WEAKENS YOU. LOSE TWO TURNS.

HARD JOURNEY OVER MOUNTAINS. REST NEEDED. LOSE A TURN.

HUNTING POOR. LACK OF FOOD WEAKENS TRIBE. LOSE A TURN.

# Barbarian Name Tags

**HUNS**

**HUNS**

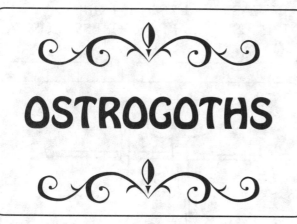

**OSTROGOTHS**

**OSTROGOTHS**

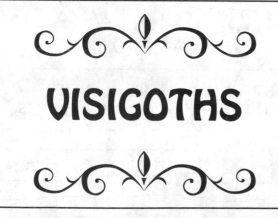

**VISIGOTHS**

**VISIGOTHS**

**VANDALS**

**VANDALS**

# Barbarian Migration (100–500 A.D.)

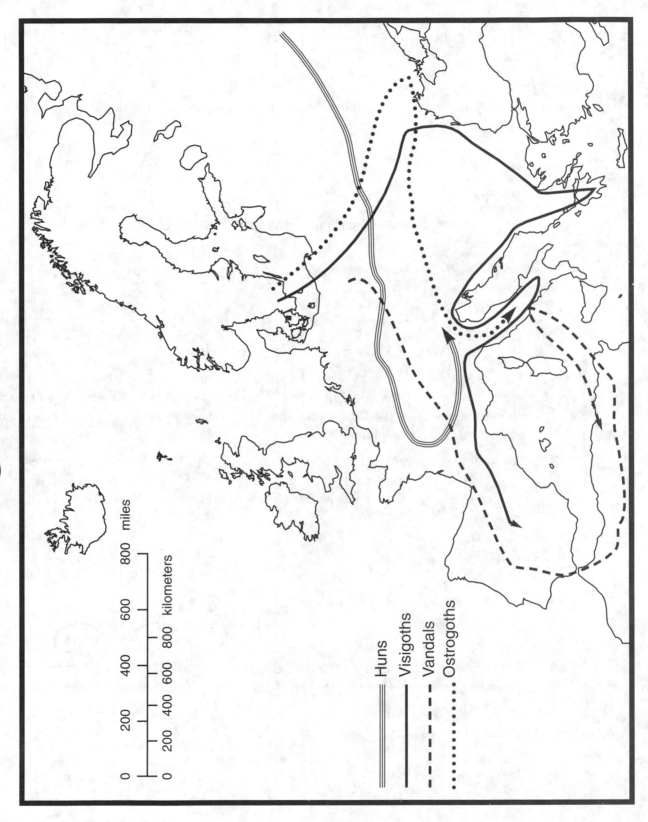

Huns
Visigoths
Vandals
Ostrogoths

800 miles

800 kilometers

200   400   600   800   kilometers

0   200   400   600   800   miles

# Latin Games

## Topic

Medieval Education: the use of Latin

## Objective

Students will identify Latin as the primary language in medieval education throughout Europe.

## Materials

- drawing paper for the Picture This game
- the accompanying Latin Scavenger Hunt paper (page 32) for the Latin Scavenger Hunt game
- Words for Latin Games list (pages 30 and 31)

## Preparation

1. Depending upon the game used, obtain the necessary materials and/or make copies of the Latin Scavenger Hunt paper for interested students.

2. The teacher needs to make a list of Latin words and their English counterparts. A suggested list for the Latin games has been provided on pages 30 and 31. Depending upon the game, that list can be duplicated several times and/or have each word cut apart on separate pieces of paper.

3. For the Latin Scavenger Hunt game, the teacher will have to utilize his or her knowledge of the community to place appropriate addresses of businesses or locales that correctly fit the Latin word with each numbered item. (A phone book would be helpful for this.)

## Procedure

*Note:* In this activity, the instructor may choose from a variety of simple games that employ the Latin language as word clues.

### Charades

1. The teacher writes a Latin word on the chalkboard that describes a common item or action within the classroom. (See Words for Latin Games for a list of words.)

2. A student is chosen to whom the teacher gives the English meaning. That student must act out the word without specifically pointing to the object (if it is a noun).

3. The student who correctly guesses the word becomes the next contestant.

# Latin Games *(cont.)*

### Picture This

1. Students are placed in cooperative learning teams of four, each with a sheet of drawing paper. The Words for Latin Games list is reproduced and distributed to all the students in a random fashion.

2. Students take turns selecting a Latin word from their personal list, writing out the Latin word, and then illustrating it. The other three members of the team should be able to see the student artist at work.

3. The student within the team that is first to correctly identify the English word from the drawing will be next to illustrate a Latin word from his or her list.

### Latin Scavenger Hunt

1. The teacher selects 12 to 15 words from the given list for students to try to associate with a given address (e.g., *textilis* would be associated with an address of a clothing or fabric store).

2. Given the Latin Scavenger Hunt paper, students will have to locate each address the teacher has placed on the list to determine the meaning of the Latin word associated with the address.

## Background

Throughout the Middle Ages, from the fall of Rome to the invention of the printing press, Latin was the language of learning throughout most of Europe. It was the language of the Roman Empire and then of Christianity. However, despite the efforts of interested nobility such as Charlemagne, education remained the sole domain of those affiliated with offices of the Church or high-ranking aristocracy. The fact that few precious books, most notably the Bible, were hand copied each year made them extremely expensive and, therefore, rare. The monasteries where these manuscripts were bound into books were, indeed, the bastions of learning and the real connection to the knowledge gained during the height of Greek and Roman culture. The Roman Catholic Church usually presented its masses in Latin, a language that only its priests and officials could readily understand. The common people submitted to the services in utter faith as they were left to believe whatever the priests told them was in the Bible since they could not read and only spoke their own local language.

The teacher is in the best position to determine which of these activities would best suit his or her class. As far as multiple intelligence modalities go, Charades would fit a kinesthetic mode while Picture This would relate more to spatial intelligence. The Latin Scavenger Hunt may be best employed as an extra credit project since students would undoubtedly be reliant upon their parents to transport them around town.

# Words for Latin Games

| Latin Word | English Word |
| --- | --- |
| ager | farm |
| cibo | animal feed |
| creta | chalk |
| curia | court |
| currus | farm equipment |
| divum | sky |
| doctrina | learning |
| domus | house |
| ecclesia | church |
| fama | talk |
| fenestra | window |
| flumen | river |
| foruli | bookcase |
| lacunar | ceiling |
| lacus | lake or pond |
| later | brick |
| lectio | to read |
| liber | book |
| magister | teacher |
| medicus | physician |

# Words for Latin Games *(cont.)*

| Latin Word | English Word |
|------------|--------------|
| *mensa* | table |
| *moderor* | to measure |
| *mons* | mountain |
| *ostium* | door |
| *paries* | wall |
| *penicullus* | pencil |
| *pontus* | bridge |
| *schola* | school |
| *scribo* | write |
| *scrinium* | notebook or binder |
| *solum* | floor |
| *statua* | statue |
| *tabella* | writing tablet |
| *textilis* | cloth or fabric |
| *theatrum* | theater |
| *venenum* | drug |
| *vestitus* | clothing |
| *via* | road |
| *victualia* | food items or groceries |

# Latin Scavenger Hunt

**Directions:** Find each address below that is associated with a given Latin word. From the business or feature found at each address, see if you can give the English meaning for each Latin word.

| | Latin word | English meaning | Address |
|---|---|---|---|
| 1. | | | |
| 2. | | | |
| 3. | | | |
| 4. | | | |
| 5. | | | |
| 6. | | | |
| 7. | | | |
| 8. | | | |
| 9. | | | |
| 10. | | | |
| 11. | | | |
| 12. | | | |
| 13. | | | |
| 14. | | | |
| 15. | | | |

# Holy Roman Emperor

## Topic

Charlemagne

## Objective

Students will identify Charlemagne as the first emperor of the Holy Roman Empire and several of his major accomplishments.

## Materials

- the accompanying Holy Roman Emperor Tossup Questions (pages 36 and 37)
- a 12" x 18" (30 cm x 46 cm) piece of tagboard or drawing paper
- a two-inch (5-cm) diameter Styrofoam ball
- gold spray paint
- glue
- tape

## Preparation

1. Roll the tagboard into a tight cylinder and tape it. Glue the Styrofoam ball to one end of the cylinder. After it has dried, spray-paint the "scepter" with gold spray paint. (This scepter will be used to denote which student holds the title of "emperor" within the classroom during the activity.)

2. *Optional*: The teacher could opt to make a crown out of the tagboard and spray-paint it gold.

## Procedure

1. After students have studied the life and times of Charlemagne, split the class into cooperative learning teams of four students each. Have each team of students prepare review questions with which they will challenge other teams.

2. To begin the actual "Holy Roman Emperor" activity, each team should select one student to be its nominee for class leader or emperor.

3. The instructor orally gives this select group of students one of the tossup questions. The student who first raises his or her hand in response will be allowed to give an answer to the question. If the answer is correct, the scepter will be presented to that student to symbolize his or her status as "Holy Roman Emperor." (*Note:* An incorrect answer by the candidate for emperor would allow the teacher to choose the next student who has his or her hand up, or the teacher could opt to read another tossup question with the initial respondent disqualified from answering.)

# Holy Roman Emperor *(cont.)*

## Procedure *(cont.)*

4. The team that has one of its members as emperor will then challenge the rest of the teams with one of its review questions. All teams are eligible to answer. The first to respond with raised hands (according to the teacher) will be allowed to answer. A correct answer from this team will have the teacher give a tossup question to its candidate for emperor. Again, should the candidate reply correctly, he or she will take over the scepter and "rule" with his or her team then challenging the class. However, if the first team to respond to the challenge question is incorrect, the reigning "emperor" from the challenging team may keep the scepter by correctly answering another tossup question. If he or she responds incorrectly, all candidates for emperor are included in another tossup round where the new emperor will be determined.

5. The activity may have a predetermined time limit or question limit (the use of all tossup questions or a certain number of challenge questions from the teams). Whoever has the reign at that set time is considered the "Holy Roman Emperor." The instructor may opt to allow the "emperor" and his or her team to skip that night's homework, obtain bonus points for their accomplishments, or receive some other worthy incentive.

## Background

Western Europe in the eighth century A.D. was a dark land, divided by tribal disputes among its barbarian inhabitants. The Roman Catholic Church was spreading its influence in the region as the major religion; yet Rome was weak. This was not the Rome of the Caesars. The Byzantine Empire (the eastern half of the former Roman Empire) threatened to try to control it, and numerous tribes, such as the Saxons and Angles in the more remote northern regions, stubbornly refused to submit to Christianity.

Toward the end of the century, a Frankish king by the name of Charlemagne (Charles the Great) came on the scene determined to create a grand Christian empire throughout western Europe. Charlemagne took up the cause of the Church in Rome and spread Christianity from the Pyrenees well into central Europe and from the North Sea to Rome. He was more than a Christian warlord, however. He had a great fondness for learning, and in the midst of the Dark Ages, he began promoting the value of education. He set up schools that taught Latin, religion, music, literature, and mathematics. He organized a court system by which local nobles would be required to dispense real justice to their peasantry. On Christmas Day in the year 800, Charlemagne was crowned "Holy Roman Emperor" by the Pope in Rome.

34

# Holy Roman Emperor *(cont.)*

## Background *(cont.)*

The title, "Holy Roman Emperor," was appropriate since Latin (or Roman) was the language of education in Charlemagne's day because it was the language of the Church. The tossup questions emphasize this detail as candidates for emperor must identify the meaning of the Latin word within each item by catching the clues. The various teams jockeying for eventual leadership simulate the fact that Western Europe was far from a united land. Although Charlemagne achieved that goal, even while he lived, certain nobles were always plotting for ways to usurp his power. With primitive transportation and communication, Charlemagne devised a messenger system to keep him informed of the loyalty of the numerous nobles serving him. After his death in 814, his three sons split the empire but were unable to maintain control for those very reasons.

## For Discussion

- How was the game similar to Western Europe in Charlemagne's time? *(Numerous nobles were trying to overtake Charlemagne's empire. Not all peoples wanted to be part of his empire.)*

- Why do you think a Latin word appeared in each tossup question? *(Latin was the language of the Roman Catholic Church. It was the language taught by schools begun by Charlemagne.)*

# Holy Roman Emperor Tossup Questions

1. Charlemagne wanted all Germanic peoples to become *christianus*. What did he want them to be? **(Christians)**

2. The *carmen* of Roland was a legendary poem which told of a battle fought by one of Charlemagne's warriors. What is the English word for *carmen*? **(song)**

3. Charlemagne wanted the *ecclesia* and *administratio* to work together to improve the lives of the people. What two institutions in society did he want to work hand in hand? **(church and government)**

4. On Christmas Day, 800 A.D., the Pope declared Charlemagne the new Roman *imperator*. What title had Charlemagne taken? **(emperor)**

5. Charlemagne set up many law *curia* to take care of local problems throughout his empire. What would we call *curia*? **(courts)**

6. Education was a major goal of Charlemagne. He wanted the Church, in particular priests living by themselves in *abbatia*, to start schools. What is the English word for *abbatia*? **(monasteries)**

7. Schools taught subjects such as Latin, *organum, litterae,* religion, and mathematics. What are *organum* and *litterae*? **(music and literature)**

8. An *ager* usually had three different sections of fields, two of which had crops while the third remained fallow. What was an *ager*? **(farm)**

9. As much as Charlemagne loved learning, he never learned how to *scribo*. What did he never learn? **(writing)**

10. Charlemagne practiced *manus manus* every night before he went to sleep, but he never really learned this skill related to the previous question. What is it? **(handwriting)**

11. During Charlemagne's time and beyond, farmers did less work for themselves and more for the nobility. They were becoming *servus*. By what term would we recognize the overworked peasants with no land for themselves? **(serfs)**

12. Three major crops planted by farmers during this era were rye, *hordeum*, and *triticus*. What were *hordeum* and *triticus*? **(barley and wheat)**

13. The *magister* was extremely important to the success of each school. Who was he? **(teacher)**

14. The *castellum* was the home of each noble. What was it? **(castle)**

15. Wealth has often been measured by how much *aurum* a person possessed. It can be assured that most people of the Dark Ages had none whatsoever. Only the very rich nobility could own it. What is *aurum*? **(gold)**

# Holy Roman Emperor Tossup
## Questions *(cont.)*

16. Roland, Charlemagne's trusted lieutenant, was killed while returning from *Hispania*. From where was he returning? (**Spain**)

17. Who was *Carolus Magnus*? (**Charlemagne/Charles the Great**)

18. Charlemagne's *avus* was Charles Martel. What is an *avus*? (**grandfather**)

19. Charlemagne was the *fillus* of Pepin the Short. What relation was he to Pepin the Short? (**son**)

20. On Christmas Day, 800 A.D., Pope Leo III placed a *corona* on Charlemagne. What did he place upon him? (**a crown**)

21. The primary weapon of Charlemagne's soldier was the *gladius*. What was it? (**sword**)

22. The most populous group of people in Charlemagne's empire were the *pagenses*. Who were they? (**peasants**)

23. Charlemagne urged that *liber libri* be copied throughout his empire. What did he want duplicated? (**books**)

24. The adjective *sanctus* described Charlemagne as the new Roman emperor under the Christian church. What does *sanctus* mean? (**holy**)

25. The era of the Middle Ages in which Charlemagne lived has often been called *atrum* due to its relative lack of civilization. The *Atrum Ages* actually means the _____ Ages. (**Dark**)

26. *Montis* separate France from Spain. What type of physical feature are they? (**mountains**)

27. The non-Christian people that Charlemagne tried to convert, like the Saxons, were referred to as *barberus*. By what word would we call them today? (**barbarians**)

28. The wealthiest, most powerful people of Charlemagne's empire were the *patricius*. What English word would describe this privileged class upon which Charlemagne always had to keep a watchful eye so they wouldn't try to overthrow him? (**nobles**)

29. Charlemagne was concerned that *justicia* would be given to the peasants of his empire. What did he want the poor farmers to have? (**justice**)

30. Numerous *gens*, such as the Lombards and Saxons, threatened Charlemagne from time to time. What are *gens*? (**tribes**)

# Aluminum Long Ships

## Topic

Vikings

## Objective

Students will recognize that one reason for the Vikings' success as sea raiders was their shallow-draft ships that could navigate far inland on rivers.

## Materials

- one roll of aluminum foil (a 25-square foot, or 2.25 square meters, roll will service 50 students)
- a plastic tub half filled with water (if a sink is unavailable)
- 20 pennies for each pair of students
- one pair of scissors

## Preparation

Cut the foil into six-inch (15-cm) square sections with the scissors.

## Procedure

1. After having a lesson on the Vikings' fondness for raiding coastal settlements in order to obtain trade goods and other plunder, ask students the following question, "What about the Vikings' ships helped them to quickly raid coastal (and inland) settlements?" *(Their ships had shallow-draft hulls that did not ride overly low in the water. This allowed them to travel up ocean-bound rivers a significant distance to carry out their raids.)*

2. Have students work in pairs on the following problem: "Given a six-inch (15-cm) square of aluminum foil, create a basic ship design that will hold 20 pennies without sinking." The following rules are to apply:

   - No other material, besides the foil, is to be used in the construction or final design of the model ship.

   - Students may offer designs closely aligned with that of the Viking long ships, but they may diverge into any other design as long as they limit themselves to the six-inch (15-cm) square of foil.

   - If more than one design holds 20 pennies, the instructor may add pennies until the craft sinks; the design holding the most pennies may be deemed the winner.

# Aluminum Long Ships *(cont.)*

## Background

The Viking warriors of Scandinavia were the scourge of many coastal villages in the British Isles and Western and Eastern Europe as far south as the Mediterranean Sea during the ninth through twelfth centuries. With arable land at home limited by rugged topography, climate, and societal customs that gave land to only the eldest son, many Scandinavian males of the era went "a viking," or pirating. With their fierce determination, navigational skills, and swift ships, they were a menace for numerous seaside communities.

"Aluminum Long Ships" combines some physics with medieval history. Students will need time out of class to fully experiment with possible designs. Generally speaking, a broader hull in this activity will allow more weight to be evenly dispersed. This will negate the need for higher sides or gunnels. Permit a few days of testing on their own before students submit their final models.

## Extension

If you allow them a few extra materials (some clay, thin dowel and/or toothpicks, and a small piece of cloth), students can create sailing crafts. If you have a larger body of water (inflatable kiddy pool) and a windy day, a contest can be held to see which craft sails the fastest and/or farthest.

# Norse Scratchings

## Topic

Vikings

## Objectives

1. Students will identify Norse letters as runes.

2. Students will decode a simple runic message.

## Materials

- the accompanying sheet of Norse Runes (page 42)

- a 12" x 18" (30 cm x 46 cm) sheet of tagboard or drawing paper

- a grocery bag or shoebox

- a coat hanger

- tape

## Preparation

1. Make several copies of Norse Runes. (The exact number of letters needed depends on how a teacher will use them in class. See Procedure, step 3.)

2. Cut out each rune (with its English letter translation) and place the individual runes in a paper bag or shoebox.

3. On the drawing paper, create a simple message using the runes that would possibly serve as a source of motivation for students. (e.g., "Whoever reads this gets five bonus points." or "Find the treasure for you in the box under the table in the back of the room.")

4. Overlap the paper onto the lower end of the coat hanger and secure it with tape.

## Procedure

1. A week before you begin a unit on the Vikings, hang the runic message in a prominent position in the classroom where each student can easily view it. (If you really want it to be obvious, use larger paper and colored markers.) The instructor should defer any questions about the strange markings until he or she is ready to present a lesson on Viking runes. However, as interest is aroused, have students hypothesize what the symbols may represent.

2. When the unit on the Vikings begins, tell the class that periodically you will be distributing letter codes that will be useful in decoding the strange message that has been hanging in the classroom for the past week. Explain that whoever is first to decode the message will be pleasantly surprised.

# Norse Scratchings *(cont.)*

## Procedure *(cont.)*

3. Letter translations should be chosen at random by a simple draw from the shoebox or grocery bag. These individual letter decoders may be given away to individual students who answer a question correctly in class, to any student who completes a homework assignment, to a cooperative team that answers correctly in a review format, or for any other circumstance the classroom teacher wishes to use.

4. The first student to turn in the exact message on a piece of paper to the teacher will be deemed the winner.

## Background

The Norse alphabet, or Futhark as it was called, was a series of 23 straight-lined symbols the Vikings employed as an alphabet. They were straight lines because the Vikings carved them into stone or wood, and curved lines would have been difficult. Viking runes were the source for spells and charms, as well as simple, everyday messages.

Viking sagas, or legendary stories, were not written down in this script. They were oral traditions that only ended up on paper several hundred years after the apex of Viking culture. When they were written down, they were written in Latin.

## Extension

• Have interested students research the Kensington Stone, a stone with apparent runic carvings on it unearthed in Kensington, Minnesota, in 1898. Its authenticity is the source of great debate among Norse scholars.

• Give students individual copies of the Futhark and have them make simple messages.

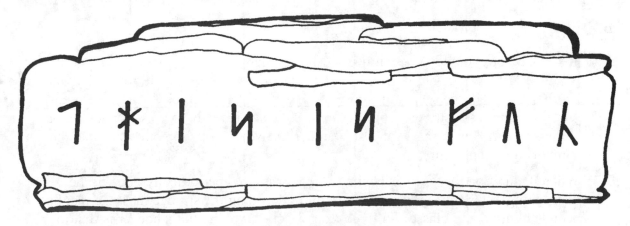

**"This is fun."**

# Norse Runes

| | | | | | |
|---|---|---|---|---|---|
| A | B | C | D | E | F |
| G | H | I/J | K | L | M |
| N | O | P | Q | R | S |
| T | U/V/W | X | Y | Z | |

# Trader Olaf

## Topic

Vikings

## Objective

Students will experiment with bartering and identify it as one method for economic transactions employed by the Vikings.

## Materials

- 1 lb. (450 g) bag of chocolate kisses (with the silver foil)
- 1 lb. (450 g) box of wheat crackers
- 1 lb. (450 g) box of "fish" crackers
- 1 lb. (450 g) box of animal-shaped cookies or crackers
- 1 lb. (450 g) bag of spice jells or gumdrops
- box of resealable, plastic sandwich bags
- thin, latex glove for each student team
- simple measuring balances (a number equal to half the number of teams in the class)
- the accompanying Varangian Trading Log (page 46)

## Preparation

1. Using a latex glove, divide the contents of the various foodstuffs into plastic bags in the following manner:

   There should be a number of plastic bags full of the "fish" crackers, wheat crackers, spice jells, and animal cookies that equals half the number of student teams within the class (three or four bags of each).

   The bags of chocolate kisses should be divided into a number of bags equal to the total number of student teams in the class (six, seven, or eight).

2. Obtain the gloves (which student handlers will wear to distribute the food in this activity) and balances. A school's science or math department may have basic measuring devices. If they are not available, simple balances can be made by using sturdy straws, string, and small plastic-mesh baskets—the kind in which small fruit, such as berries, are packaged. Tie the baskets to each end of a straw, and tie the string in the center of the straw to hold the balance.

3. Make enough copies of the Varangian Trading Log to have one for each team.

# Trader Olaf *(cont.)*

## Procedure

1. Students should be in cooperative teams of four each. Each team member will have a role to fulfill.

   • A *Trader* will conduct trades of products between his or her team and another.

   • A *Master Measurer* will be in charge of weighing all items to ensure a fair trade.

   • A *Scribe* will record all transactions in the official Varangian Trading Log.

   • Finally, a *Bearer* will be responsible for transporting goods from station to station.

2. Divide the various teams into either Viking trading groups or Byzantine traders (an equal number of each).

3. Distribute the one bag of "fish" crackers, one bag of animal cookies, and one bag of chocolate kisses to each Viking team.

4. Give one bag of spice jells or gumdrops, one bag of wheat crackers, and one bag of chocolate kisses to the Byzantine traders.

5. Number each team (or have them name themselves) and arrange a trading order to ensure that each Viking group will have three trading sessions (of several minutes each)—two with separate Byzantine groups and one with another Viking group.

6. Instruct students that they will be engaging in a trading simulation wherein each person has a role, as outlined in #1. Viking teams will take their goods with them when visiting Byzantine teams. One person from each team will handle negotiating trades (*Trader*); one will ensure fair measure (*Master Measurer*); one will record transactions (*Scribe*); one will transport goods (*Bearer*). (See Background on the next page for symbolic meanings of the various foodstuffs.)

7. Each team's objective should be to complete successful trades with at least two other groups. Balances are to be used to ensure equal trades, and the *Master Measurer* must wear a latex glove when transferring food items.

## Background

The Vikings were known as fierce pirates/raiders and for good reason. They were a scourge along northern coasts of Europe. They worked their way as far south as the Black Sea and the Mediterranean. However, the Norsemen were as shrewd as they were vicious. If an intended victim of a raid seemed too strong to be terrorized by Viking force, the ancient Scandinavians went to an alternate plan to get what they wanted—barter.

# Trader Olaf *(cont.)*

## *Background (cont.)*

Along the Varangian Trade Route which ran southward from the Baltic to the Black Sea and into Constantinople, Vikings exported animal hides, slaves, jewelry, and fish for commodities more prevalent around Asia Minor and the Balkan peninsula (the approximate location of the Byzantine Empire, the eastern half of the former Roman Empire)—wheat, gold, spices, wine, and silk.

In Trader Olaf, the various foods/candies employed are symbolic of many of these former trade goods. Using "fish" crackers (fish), animal cookies (animal hides), spice jells or gumdrops (spices), wheat crackers (wheat), and chocolate kisses (silver) is an attempt to engage students in the barter method in Viking trade.

Chunks of silver and gold coins were used in these trades as a measure of weight equal to a certain amount of goods in return. Gold-foiled chocolates could, therefore, also be used. Perhaps several sets of weights could be borrowed from the science or math department of your school, and students could arrange trades based on certain standard or metric weights of agreed-upon items.

# Varangian Trading Log

| ITEMS TRADED | GOODS RECEIVED |
|---|---|
| _____ | _____ |
| _____ | _____ |
| _____ | _____ |
| _____ | _____ |
| _____ | _____ |
| _____ | _____ |
| _____ | _____ |
| _____ | _____ |
| _____ | _____ |
| _____ | _____ |
| _____ | _____ |
| _____ | _____ |
| _____ | _____ |
| _____ | _____ |
| _____ | _____ |

# Unbridled Resolve

## Topic

Early Islam

## Objective

Students will explain how the religion of Islam spread as quickly and as far as it did.

## Materials

None are required.

## Preparation

None is required.

## Procedure

1. Prior to initiating a unit or chapter on the origins of Islam, divide students into cooperative learning teams. Explain to the class that if they work diligently and cooperatively, they will receive a reward.

2. Assign five questions for students to answer. These questions may be review questions from previously learned material, or they may concern initial readings about the religion of Islam.

3. Explain to the class that to begin, each student is to answer each question using complete sentences (so that each answer will be very explicit and clearly understood by the instructor). Each student's paper is to be labeled with a number from one to four (corresponding with the four members of the team) instead of a name.

4. After students have answered the questions as individuals, they are to share results and discuss the questions with one partner from their team. Subsequently, they are to share and discuss answers with the other pair of students within their team.

5. Each student should then take his or her answers to one other team and continue the process of sharing and discussing. They are to return to their team for one final review of the five answers. In this final review, they are to rewrite any answers that need to be corrected so each student has what he or she believes are the correct answers in complete sentence form.

6. With about 10 minutes of class remaining, the teacher will randomly collect one paper from each team, selecting a particular paper (#1, #2, #3, #4) from that group. The teacher will grade each of the five to seven papers collected. If all answers are correct, the teacher will distribute the reward.

# Unbridled Resolve *(cont.)*

## Procedure *(cont.)*

7. As closure for this particular day's lesson or as an introduction to a subsequent lesson on the origin of the Islamic religion, the instructor should direct the students' attention on the emotional dynamics of the review question lesson.

   - "Did you approach answering these questions any differently from other review questions you've been given?"

   - "Were you able to work more cooperatively with your classmates than you usually do? Why or why not?"

   - "What was the major reason you may have been more motivated in this activity?"

8. Lead students into discussing how the Islamic religion spread out of Arabia in the seventh and eighth centuries A.D. (See Background.) Through questions similar to the following ones, lead students to see the analogous relationship between their drive to get the reward and the determined resolve of the followers of Islam:

   - "What was similar between your work on the five-question review assignment and the Muslims' spread of their religion?" *(Both were worthwhile goals for the people involved.)*

   - "How did people work to achieve these goals?" *(Muslims were absolutely united and convinced of the righteousness of their cause. Students may have been extremely motivated to get the reward and so worked well together on their review questions.)*

## Background

From the time of Mohammed's revelation from God, 610 A.D. to about 750 A.D., the fervor of Islam spread across Arabia throughout the present-day Middle East, moving eastward to India and westward into Spain and southern France. It was able to travel like the wind due to a united, almost fanatical, people devoted to the beliefs of their religion and willing to die for it. Serving their God with these convictions earned a Muslim a place in Paradise after death.

While no simulated effort can produce such conviction, students should realize the heightened effort they placed in their classwork when a significant goal was perceived as attainable. This line of reasoning makes all the more fantastic, the accomplishments of the early Muslims as they embarked on their mission with blind faith.

# An Irresistible Offer?

## Topic

The Byzantine Empire

## Objective

Students will identify inducements the emperor Constantine offered people to move to his fledgling capital city of Constantinople and compare similar situations offered by the American government in our history and by local governments for business purposes today.

## Materials

- the accompanying Team Goal Contract (page 52)

- one bag of candy or multi-pack of gum

(*Note:* Food rewards need not be employed. Bonus points or other reinforcers may be used.)

## Preparation

1. Make one copy of the contract for each team in the class.

2. Obtain the reward.

## Procedure

1. Have students divide into cooperative learning teams of about four students each. Lay out the bag of candy or gum in plain view of the entire class. (You may even partake of it in order to better set the tone of your announcement.) Explain to the class, "I'm going to make a deal with each team today. The team that follows through on their deal with me will walk away with this goodie bag."

2. The "deal" is this. Each team is to discuss what it thinks each member could possibly score on the next chapter or unit test. Prompt students by pointing out that individual goals should be relatively high but realistically attainable. The team should then use the Team Goal Contract to list each individual member's name, his or her goal, and the team's subsequent average goal.

3. The teacher is to collect the Team Goal Contract from each team and announce what each team has offered in return for the reward. It is important to stress that what is offered is not a deal until the goal has actually been met. The team that meets the highest goal will be rewarded.

4. After all student questions concerning the deal have been discussed, the teacher will use the offer as an introduction to the Byzantium Empire. Discuss Constantine's founding of Constantinople and see if students are able to compare his offers (See Background.) to events in our nation's past or present.

# An Irresistible Offer? *(cont.)*

## Procedure *(cont.)*

5. Encourage student teams to form study groups outside of class as much as possible and to use class time to its fullest in order to reach their desired goal. Remind them that it makes no difference if another team has a higher goal if that group of students doesn't reach it. Emphasize that team members should encourage each other. Each individual can control how much effort he or she puts into preparing for the chapter or unit test.

## Background

In 330 A.D., the Roman emperor Constantine moved his capital out of Rome and into the old Asia Minor city of Byzantium along the Bosporous Strait, which connects the Black Sea with the Sea of Marmara and, ultimately, the Aegean Sea. He quadrupled the size of old Byzantium and renamed it Constantinople in his honor. Constantine, who was the first emperor of Rome to embrace Christianity, did build a few churches in his new city. However, numerous other reasons could be given to explain his abandonment of Rome. His new location was along established and well-protected trade routes; the eastern half of the Roman Empire was materially better off than the west; Germanic invaders were more prevalent in the west; political intrigue was rampant in Rome.

To help build his city and give it credibility, Constantine offered inducements for many to follow him to Constantinople. He offered to build palaces for wealthy patricians if they relocated to Constantinople. He also offered large tracts of land and annual payments of grain for numerous years to come.

Although Constantine's offer met with very limited success, Constantinople grew into an extremely prosperous city, which remained the secure headquarters of the eastern Roman Empire (later named the Byzantine Empire) until its fall to the Ottoman Turks in 1453. Noted for a variety of trading enterprises and other businesses, its populace was well educated. Meanwhile, Rome, having been sacked several times by barbarians in the fifth century A.D., retreated into the backwater of history.

Much of the United States was settled in a somewhat similar fashion through the Homestead Act of 1862, which opened up vast areas of the Great Plains. One notable difference is that those that homesteaded the American frontier were usually of a lower economic class who would not normally have been able to afford the land.

In the present day, however, a different sort of deal is often reported in newspapers nationwide. Tax abatements are offered by municipal and county governments to lure various industries and their employment opportunities into their communities. Derided by some as "corporate welfare" and praised by others who view the jobs created or saved by such practices as absolutely necessary, tax abatement is somewhat analogous to Constantine's offer of almost two thousand years ago. Constantine counted upon relocating wealthy Romans to add to the stature and economic stability of his new capital.

# An Irresistible Offer? *(cont.)*

## Extensions

- Have students research the Homestead Act. They may write a report or create a display board. This may be very appropriate if students live in that part of the country where the Homestead Act was the means for settling the frontier.

- Students may also focus on current events. Interested students could bring in newspaper articles about local tax abatement issues. Perhaps informed speakers could offer pro and con arguments on the issue. Students themselves might be able to research the topic (if it is newsworthy enough in their area) and have a classroom debate on it.

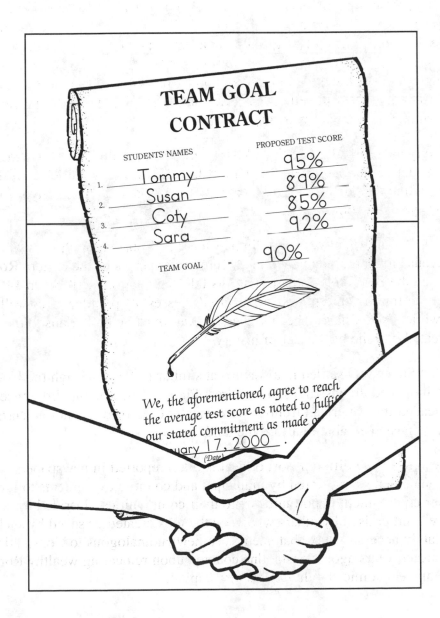

# TEAM GOAL
# CONTRACT

STUDENTS' NAMES                          PROPOSED TEST SCORE

1. _____        _____

2. _____        _____

3. _____        _____

4. _____        _____

TEAM GOAL          =          _____

We, the aforementioned, agree to reach
the average test score as noted to fulfill
our stated commitment as made on

_____ .

(Date)

# Icon Adoration

## Topic

The Byzantine Empire

## Objective

Students will recognize icon worship as one source of division between the early Roman Catholic Church and the Orthodox Church of the Byzantine Empire.

## Materials

- the accompanying Icon Adoration Symbols sheets (pages 55 and 56)
- an overhead and transparencies for each of the pictographs

## Preparation

Make an overhead transparency of each of the pictographs on the accompanying sheets.

## Procedure

1. While engaged in the study of a unit on the Byzantine Empire, surprise students at the beginning of the class period with the announcement of a "pop" quiz. They need to get out a sheet of paper and number it one to five.

2. The quiz will consist of each of the five pictograph transparencies that students will try to identify by correctly naming them on their papers.

3. When the last of the pictographs has been displayed, collect the quizzes. Then survey students as to their opinions of the quiz: "What did you like about the quiz?" "What was unusual about the quiz format?" "Did you think it was fair?" "Would you like future quizzes like this one if they weren't surprise quizzes?"

4. The intent of the previous questions is to hopefully engender a discussion where the class presents diverse points of view regarding the quiz's symbolic nature. Those students who are more visual learners may have liked to take the pictographs quiz. Other students may very well have resented being evaluated on the basis of symbols they did not create or that had not been previously reviewed.

    Assure students that the quiz will not count as a grade. Rather, use the simulation as an introduction for a lesson on one of the divisions that developed between the Church of the Western Roman Empire (Roman Catholic) and the Church of the Eastern Roman Empire, or Byzantine Empire (Greek Orthodox). (See Background.)

# Icon Adoration *(cont.)*

## Background

In the eighth century A.D., many Christians in the former Roman Empire used icons, or religious images, to assist in their worship services. In the Byzantine Empire (the eastern half of the former Roman Empire centered in Constantinople), disagreements developed as to whether or not icons broke the second commandment which prohibited the making of "graven images."

While the emperor of the Byzantine Empire tried to wrestle his people away from icon worship, the leaders of the Roman Church in Italy became upset with the Byzantines. Since most people in Western Europe at this time could not read, icons were valuable assets in teaching Christianity. The Pope and other church leaders in Rome summarily dismissed the Byzantine emperor from the Christian church.

Even though the Byzantine emperor eventually allowed his people to keep icons in their worship, the rift that originated between the eastern and western branches of Christianity over icon worship grew wider and wider with each century. By the middle of the eleventh century, the Roman Catholic Church and the Greek Orthodox Church were completely separate entities.

## Extension

Pictographs can be a unique way for students to visualize the meanings of various terms. Having students create their own pictographs and sharing them with classmates is a refreshingly different way to review vocabulary.

---

### Answers to icons on pages 55 and 56

Teachers may wish to substitute their own icons for this simulation. The ones included in this activity are as follows:

1. doctrine (religious teachings)
2. Greek fire (flames used by the Byzantines in warfare, that couldn't be put out with water)
3. dowry (money brought into a marriage by the bride)
4. patriarch (leading church official of the Eastern Orthodox Church)
5. emperor (chief religious, governmental, and military leader of the Byzantine Empire)

---

# Icon Adoration Symbols

1.

2.

3.

# Icon Adoration Symbols *(cont.)*

4.

5.

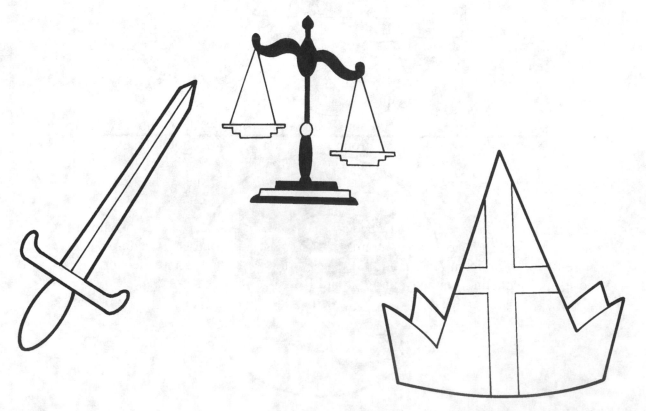

56

# Theodora— Phenomenal First Lady

## Topic

The Byzantine Empire

## Objectives

1. Students will identify the accomplishments of Empress Theodora of the Byzantine Empire.

2. *Optional*: They will compare and contrast her accomplishments with those of recent American first ladies.

## Materials

- one copy of the accompanying story starter, A Desperate Emperor (page 59), for each student

## Preparation

Make sufficient copies of A Desperate Emperor.

## Procedure

1. As an introduction to a lesson on Byzantine emperor Justinian and his wife Theodora, pass out the story starter, A Desperate Emperor, to each student. Read through the text orally with the class or have them read it silently.

2. Have students write a one- to two-paragraph conclusion to the story starter in which students imagine Theodora's response to the conflict at hand. Even though the students will not have been exposed to Theodora's character at this time, they should try to offer reasoning for how Theodora responds in their story's completion. (This may be an overnight assignment or done in class.)

3. After students have finished their endings, allow time for class discussion. Whether or not discussion is preceded by small group interaction, students should be exposed to the ideas expressed by various classmates. Those ideas should be weighed as to which endings might be most probable, given the setting and circumstances of Justinian's dilemma.

4. Begin the lesson on Justinian and Theodora. (See Background.) If there is enough time, students can create Venn diagrams that compare and contrast Theodora's reign as empress with prominent American first ladies of this century, such as Eleanor Roosevelt, Jacqueline Kennedy, and Barbara Bush.

# Theodora—
# Phenomenal First Lady *(cont.)*

## Background

Empress Theodora was a most unusual lady. Born poor, she became an actress in her teens. Actresses were seen as somewhat contemptible, and there was even a law that prohibited an emperor from marrying such a woman. However, Justinian's heart overruled his legal sense, and he had the law rewritten so he could marry Theodora. She did not disappoint her emperor.

She helped Justinian fill critical government and church positions. She worked for women's rights by advocating that women could own land and that daughters born of slaves weren't to be automatically considered slaves. She had hospitals built for the poor and established a home for vagrant women. Under her direction, daughters received equal inheritance with sons.

While Justinian suffered the ill effects of plague for several months, Theodora ruled the Byzantine Empire. In short, Theodora and Justinian shared an almost joint reign.

In the tense situation outlined in A Desperate Emperor, Theodora spoke boldly about a ruler's right and duty to lead by example, even if that meant possible death. Leaving Constantinople would only energize the forces opposed to Justinian. Theodora's speech swayed Justinian and his council. Under the lead of his military commanders, 30,000 insurgents were killed in the ensuing days of fighting, and Justinian held onto the throne.

Interestingly, most of Justinian's achievements as an emperor, including the law code that bears his name, came with Theodora at his side. After her death in 548 A.D., not much of significance is attributed to Justinian in his final 16 years of rule.

# A Desperate Emperor

## Constantinople, 532 A.D.

The crowd at the Hippodrome in Constantinople had been in an agitated state since it arrived around midday. While they were there for the customary chariot races, more pressing business would be conducted this afternoon. Large numbers of two opposing religious groups, the Blues and the Greens, were in attendance, hurling insults at each other and at Emperor Justinian. With rising taxes annoying the rich and diminished government services angering the poor, the rest of the crowd would soon throw their voices against the emperor just as the conniving leaders from each religious camp had hoped. Their emotions at a boil, like so many maddened hornets in a disturbed nest, the crowd took advantage of a lull in the races and rushed toward the center of the oval and toppled a
statue of Justinian. From there they spilled out into the city, spreading their venom amongst the masses. Soon tens of thousands were in open revolt. The Blues and Greens had each named a new emperor to give legitimacy to their respective causes. Fires were being set, property was being destroyed—Constantinople, the capital of the Byzantine Empire, was in total chaos.

Meanwhile, word reached Justinian that massive riots had broken out. His advisors urged Justinian to flee Constantinople in order to possibly regroup his forces for an eventual counterattack. Surely, all their lives were in grave danger should they remain. As he listened anxiously to his council, Justinian was about to render his decision when he was interrupted by his wife, the Empress Theodora. Concern etched on her face from her slightly wrinkled brow to her narrow pursed lips, Theodora spoke.

**Directions:** Write one or two paragraphs on what you think Theodora, the emperor's wife, may have said at this extremely dangerous time.

_____

_____

_____

_____

_____

_____

_____

# A Puzzling Situation

## Topic

Medieval Feudalism

## Objective

Students will recognize that feudal Europe of the intermediary Middle Ages was made up of nominally-sized kingdoms that included hundreds of feudal estates bound in a very loose confederation.

## Materials

- the accompanying Map of France (page 62)
- a number of resealable, plastic sandwich bags equal to the number of cooperative learning teams within the class

## Preparation

1. Make enough copies of the map so that there are two for each team of students.
2. Take half of the maps and cut up each map into small pieces. Place the pieces of each map in a separate plastic bag.

## Procedure

1. Distribute a complete map of France to the various student teams.

2. Then distribute the dissected maps of France in the plastic bags, one per team. Instruct students to piece this map puzzle together using the full map of France as a guide. (Students will probably give you an incredulous look upon opening the bags and with good reason! Allow a few minutes of struggle before calling a halt to the "puzzle mania." It will only frustrate students to go longer, especially since the point will have been made.)

3. Explain to the class that one thousand years ago in Western Europe alone, feudal estates numbered in the thousands. While there were numerous kingdoms to which any particular estate may have professed loyalty, there was no concept of nations or of a single country that had expansive borders. The bag full of map pieces represents how a map of France (or most any European territory) in 1000 A.D. may have appeared with each small piece a separate feudal estate. The power of the king depended upon the willingness of the various nobles to give him loyalty in the form of food and soldiers for his army. With so many nobles existing with their own armies, the power of the kingdom was often in doubt. Nobles even minted their own coins!

# A Puzzling Situation *(cont.)*

## Background

After the death of Charlemagne in 814 A.D., his Holy Roman Empire fell into a state of disorder with local nobles basically having free rein governing their immediate locales. With the danger brought on by the Vikings in the tenth century, feudalism (the concept of loyalty and food for protection) grew steadily.

There were, as mentioned, a number of loosely confederated kingdoms based upon language. However, the connection within these kingdoms came primarily from the nobility who owed military loyalty and food to higher ranking lords. Each controlled an estate which measured about a few hundred square miles. It was as if the state of New York would have been a kingdom whose king had power only if the nobles (who controlled each separate county within the state) were willing to give it to him. The common peasant took his orders directly from his estate's lord who dictated all rules of the estate. Life was harsh for the commoner.

It wasn't until 1314 that France united under one ruler, Philip IV. This only took place after a national legislature, the Estates-General, had been established in order to offer representation for the various estates on matters of national importance. Similarly, the Parliament in England developed in the latter half of the thirteenth century.

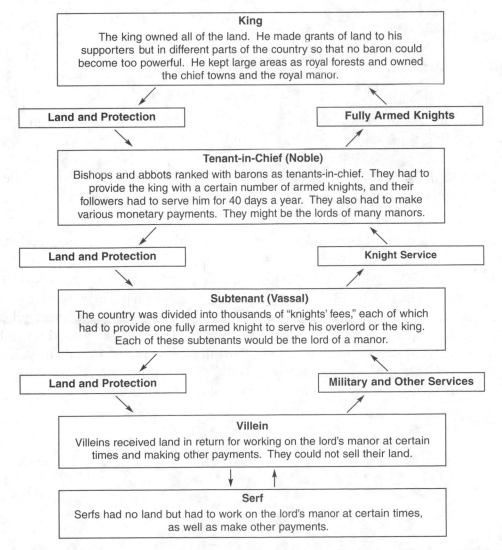

**King**
The king owned all of the land. He made grants of land to his supporters but in different parts of the country so that no baron could become too powerful. He kept large areas as royal forests and owned the chief towns and the royal manor.

**Land and Protection**      **Fully Armed Knights**

**Tenant-in-Chief (Noble)**
Bishops and abbots ranked with barons as tenants-in-chief. They had to provide the king with a certain number of armed knights, and their followers had to serve him for 40 days a year. They also had to make various monetary payments. They might be the lords of many manors.

**Land and Protection**      **Knight Service**

**Subtenant (Vassal)**
The country was divided into thousands of "knights' fees," each of which had to provide one fully armed knight to serve his overlord or the king. Each of these subtenants would be the lord of a manor.

**Land and Protection**      **Military and Other Services**

**Villein**
Villeins received land in return for working on the lord's manor at certain times and making other payments. They could not sell their land.

**Serf**
Serfs had no land but had to work on the lord's manor at certain times, as well as make other payments.

# Map of France

62

# Feudal Classroom

## Topic

Medieval Feudalism

## Objectives

1. Students will identify the various ranks of feudal society.

2. Students will work to improve in a specific academic area.

## Materials

- the accompanying certificates (pages 66 and 67)

## Preparation

Depending upon the improvement goal the teacher is going to propose, previous averages in this area will have to be determined. (e.g., If the goal is for students to raise their social studies tests averages, the average of the current or previous grading period's social studies tests needs to be calculated for each student.)

## Procedure

1. Students need to be introduced to the social strata prevalent in European feudalism. (See Background.)

2. Students will work in cooperative learning teams. The teacher will select a specific, quantifiable goal that he or she deems worthy for student improvement. In a self-contained classroom, the goal may involve improvement in several subject areas. In a departmentalized setting, social studies tests, completion of and accuracy on homework assignments, project performance, etc., may be the definitive areas in which students are expected to improve their performances.

3. For each student, the teacher will calculate an existing average for the predetermined task. Each team will then also have a predetermined average based upon its members' averages. The teacher will set an improvement goal for which student teams will rise in feudal rank if that goal is obtained. (e.g., Teams increasing their test average by 5% will receive the rank of "Vassal"; those teams raising scores 10% will receive the rank of "High Noble.") Teams not reaching the prescribed goals will remain in "Peasant" classification. There should be no need for the use of a "Serf" category.

# Feudal Classroom *(cont.)*

## Procedure *(cont.)*

4. Students will have greater motivation if certain privileges are accorded to the various ranks. Each teacher will be in the best position to determine what reinforcers will work best with his or her students. The following are possible incentives:

   - food
   - being excused from class first
   - free homework pass (good for one assignment)
   - bonus points
   - longer recess
   - special activity period
   - a special letter of recognition sent home to parents
   - presentation of the accompanying merit certificates

5. *Optional*: So that individual students are not discouraged by poorly motivated team members, an individual ranking system may also be employed. In this system, teams and individuals who attain the set goals are awarded the designated incentives. Again, each teacher is the best judge as to whether this combined system would be optimal for his or her classroom.

## Background

The king (or queen) was, theoretically, the highest ranking person within a kingdom. However, in medieval Europe, many kings were dependent upon powerful nobles for military loyalty and for food. These nobles had lesser nobles, known as vassals, subservient to them. Vassals owed military loyalty and food to the higher nobility. Land ownership was tied to military service. Land ownership was the means to attaining wealth and power in medieval Europe.

Toward the bottom of this social pyramid lay the peasants, poor freedmen, who eked out a living by farming the land. At the very bottom rung of the societal ladder were the serfs and peasants who were bound to the land and who were part and parcel of it when it was sold from one noble to another. These lower two classes grew the food that allowed the privileged few the time and energy to govern and protect the masses.

In the "Feudal Classroom," reaching improvement goals is the means to attaining certain privileges.

# Feudal Classroom *(cont.)*

## Background *(cont.)*

One question that always arises when pursuing improvement goals with students deals with those high achieving students who regularly score in the ninetieth percentile. Using mathematical reasoning, one can recognize that improvement at this level is difficult to attain. One possible solution is as follows: Students who presently average at 95% and higher are accorded the highest rank ("High Noble") for maintaining that level of performance. Students presently scoring between 90–94% will receive the title of "Vassal" for maintaining that level, but scoring at 95% or higher will raise them to the title of "High Noble." For other students, the instructor needs to incorporate the percentage increase he or she deems most appropriate.

The "Feudal Classroom" should continue throughout the entire time spent on the Middle Ages. Each individual teacher is in the best position to determine what quantifiable task is most critically in need of student improvement.

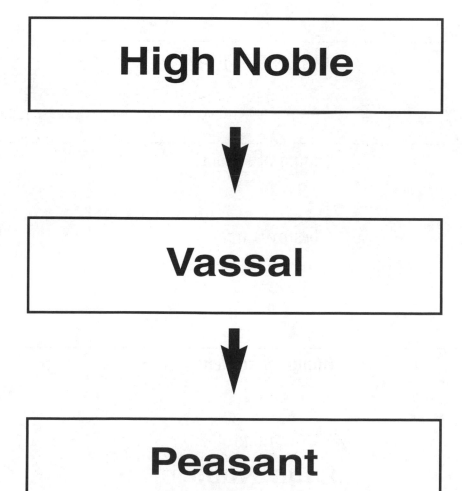

# High Noble Achievement Certificate

In honor of meritorius achievement and by decree of the most high

majesty,_____ of

(last name of teacher)

_____

(name of school)

bestows upon

_____

(name of student)

the rank of

## High Noble

with all its accompanying privileges.

# Vassal Achievement Certificate

In honor of meritorius achievement and by decree of the most high

majesty,_____ of

(last name of teacher)

_____

(name of school)

bestows upon

_____

(name of student)

the rank of

**Vassal**

with all its accompanying privileges.

# Academic Joust

## Topic

Medieval Feudalism

## Objectives

1. Students will identify the purpose of a medieval jousting tournament.

2. Students will review important concepts and information prior to a test.

## Materials

- a small box or container

## Preparation

1. Obtain a container.

2. For Academic Joust, prepare to review previously presented material relating to medieval studies.

## Procedure

1. Prior to testing students on medieval information, place students in cooperative learning teams. Discuss with students the purposes of and events within a medieval tournament for knights, especially the joust. (See Background.)

2. For an assignment, each team is to create a number of review questions for the material covered in class instruction on medieval life. The teacher should determine exactly how many questions are to be made. They may include multiple choice items, fill-ins, or direct answer questions.

3. At the time of the actual "joust," each team should be numbered or named. The teams' numbers or names should be placed in a container of some sort. The teacher proceeds to select one team (the "Challenger") from the container. The "Challenger" will ask a question of the second team (the "Challenged") chosen from the container by the teacher.

4. If the "Challenger's" question is answered correctly by the second team, the "Challenged" scores five points. However, if they are incorrect, the challenging team scores five points. The teacher will then draw one more team name/number from the container to be challenged by the same question with similar scoring. If the question hasn't been answered correctly after the second "joust," the answer should be given.

# Academic Joust *(cont.)*

## Procedure *(cont.)*

5.  At this point, the teacher selects two new names from the container and follows the procedure outlined in steps 3 and 4. When less than two team names are left in the container, replace all cards and start anew.

## Background

Tournaments were events that combined military skills and athleticism within the context of a social gathering during the Middle Ages. Nobility came and observed the contests that were usually held in a large, open field. The joust was the most notable skill event, pitting two men on horseback riding at each other, each armed with a long lance with the intent of knocking one's opponent off his horse. While many jousts were just a sporting event with padded lance points, some were in deadly earnest, using sharp weapons. In the latter, the victorious combatant claimed his deceased opponent's weapons, which he could sell.

The "Academic Joust" uses the idea of a challenge to motivate students to greater preparedness for their upcoming examination.

# Pulling the Wool

## Topic

The Crusades

## Objective

Students will explain how the Crusades began with the plea and promises from Pope Urban II.

## Materials

- the accompanying dilemma, Skin-Flint Enterprises, on page 73

## Preparation

Make sufficient copies of Skin-Flint Enterprises so each student has one.

## Procedure

1. Have students situated in cooperative learning teams of four students each. Distribute copies of the vignette Skin-Flint Enterprises. Have students read it.

2. Students should discuss the follow-up questions within their own team for approximately three or four minutes before whole class discussion ensues to allow for everyone to verbalize their thoughts on this very unusual story.

3. Engage the entire class in a discussion of Skin-Flint Enterprises. Along with the follow-up questions (possible answers given on page 72), other appropriate questions for the class may include the following:

   - "Could such an occurrence ever happen in reality? Why or why not?"

   - "What do you think of Mr. Skinner and Mr. Flint from the limited context of this story?"

   - "Do you think it was ethical for Mr. Skinner and Mr. Flint to approach their community with this request without revealing the entire plan?"

4. Have students begin their reading on the origins of the Crusades. Discuss with them the analogous relationship between these beginnings of religious war and Skin-Flint Enterprises. (See Background.) Use the following discussion questions:

   - "What was the conflict that developed toward the end of the eleventh century?" (*Moslem Seljuq Turks conquered the Holy Land, making it difficult for Christian pilgrims to worship at shrines and were threatening the Byzantine Empire, a Christian political unit.*)

   - "What problem existed in the story, Skin-Flint Enterprises?" (*An abandoned, yet historic hotel was going to be torn down to make way for office space.*)

# Pulling the Wool *(cont.)*

## *Procedure (cont.)*

    4. *(cont.)*

- "What powerful leader came asking for help of the people?" *(Pope Urban II)*

- "Who came asking for help for saving the hotel, and whom did they ask?" *(Mr. Skinner and Mr. Flint, two local businessmen got support from the community for help.)*

- "What did the Pope want the people to do?" *(He wanted them to travel to the Holy Land to fight the Muslims and drive them out.)*

- "What did the two businessmen want members of their community to do?" *(First they urged people to petition the county commissioners to save the hotel. Then they convinced members of the community to invest in their renovation of the hotel.)*

- "What promises did the Pope make to motivate people?" *(He said debts would be forgiven, serfs could gain freedom, nobles could gain land and homes, and all who died in battle would be forgiven of their sins.)*

- "What promises did Mr. Skinner and Mr. Flint make?" *(Investors would increase the amount of their investment ten times in just about a year after the hotel reopened.)*

- "What might Skinner and Flint's plan have cost the people of Humboldt? *(It may have cost some investors money while the community itself could have been unhappy with a gambling casino in its downtown.)*

- "What did Pope Urban II's plea cost Christian Europe?" *(While students will obviously not be cognizant of the particulars, they should be able to realize that years of war and many deaths were the result.)*

## *Background*

Pulling the Wool uses the all-to-common premise of the business scheme to effectively alert students to the very cause of the Crusades. In 1071, Moslem Seljuq Turks captured the Holy Land of Palestine. Christian shrines in and around Jerusalem were made difficult to reach for Christian pilgrims from Europe. Furthermore, the Seljuq Turks were threatening the security of the Byzantine Empire. Several times over the next 20 years, the Byzantine emperor had sought military assistance from the Pope in Rome. In 1095, Pope Urban II believed it was crucial to offer such aid.

In a speech in Clermont, France, Pope Urban II implored Frankish Christians to retake the Holy Land and drive out the Muslim invaders, the "infidels." While no exact record of his words exist, several first hand accounts indicate Urban II made numerous promises to the masses for those would take on the crusade—new homes and land in the Holy Land for nobles who, because they were not the eldest son, had none bequeathed to them; freedom for all serfs who undertook the cause; cancellation of all debts against peasants who went; and most importantly, God would forgive the sins of all who died in battle.

# Pulling the Wool *(cont.)*

## *Background (cont.)*

It is important to remember that during these medieval times, books were scarce and people who could read were even more dispersed. Reading was a privilege of the high nobility and the clergy. The Bible was read and interpreted as seen fit by the Church. If the Church hierarchy said, "God wills it," it must be so. While Urban's desire to free Christian shrines may bespeak of his devotion to his faith, the historical record also points out that he hoped to take advantage of the Byzantine Empire's cry for help.

The Eastern Orthodox Church of Constantinople had split from the Roman Catholic Church in 1054. Pope Urban II viewed the Crusade as his opportunity to reunite the two churches with himself in charge. The degree to which faith interplayed with the desire for power is debatable. However, it is fair to state both dynamics were at work in this event.

---

### Answers to questions on page 73

1. The Humboldt Hotel is being saved.

2. Over eight thousand community members signed petitions to save the hotel from the wrecking ball. Also, numerous citizens became unwitting investors in the Skin-Flint scheme.

3. Mr. Skinner and Mr. Flint are literally trying to "pull the wool over the eyes" of their community. They are taking advantage of civic pride and the community ignorance of a little known gambling law in their state to make themselves rich.

4. The investors seem so eager to make money, they apparently allow their greed to override their common sense.

5. With the context clues given that the community is a hard-working, farming center with a rich, historic tradition, it would seem unlikely that the citizenry would support a gambling establishment if they knew of the plans ahead of time.

6. Answers will vary.

---

# Skin-Flint Enterprises

Richard Skinner and Benjamin Flint, two ambitious businessmen from Humboldt, had made quite a name for themselves recently as they spearheaded a local petition drive to save the historic Humboldt Hotel. The abandoned structure, which had served its purpose well as a dignified home to visitors to this quiet county seat for over a hundred years, was to have been torn down. The county commissioners had desired to buy the hotel to use the space for much-needed government office space. The government officials thought it would have been a wise use of tax dollars for the hard-working people in this farm community. However, the outcry from the tradition-rich citizenry, which was orchestrated by Mr. Skinner and Mr. Flint, led to a petition with over eight thousand signatures. When the commissioners realized that over one-half of the voting public of their county wanted the dilapidated hotel saved, they had agreed to the restoration project managed by Skin-Flint Enterprises.

Skinner and Flint were anxiously awaiting the start of their special meeting which would initiate the second phase of a secretly ingenious plan. They had placed ads in the local newspaper for the past month announcing an opportunity to become an investor in the Humboldt Hotel Project. Tonight they would explain how, for a minimum investment of $1,000, any citizen could easily reap a ten-fold profit in about one year. Richard Skinner planted the seed, "Imagine ladies and gentlemen, one thousand dollars tonight could be turned into ten thousand dollars for you within one year of the hotel's restoration!"

Feeling the urge of a carnival barker, Ben Flint fanned the flames of greed, "With the Humboldt Hotel restored to her original architectural eloquence, visitors from far and wide will once again visit Humboldt in great numbers. Our studies indicate that the downtown business district will benefit greatly as the tourists will spend their money within a two mile radius of the hotel." Dollar signs seemingly danced in the eyes of the crowded audience. They liked what Skin-Flint was selling.

Later that same night Richard and Ben were slapping each other on the back. Over one-and-a-half million dollars had been extracted from the crowd in their first public meeting. With two more meetings to go, their prospects were looking good. It looked like their plan would work to perfection. The good citizens of Humboldt would raise the money to restore the old hotel, and then Skin-Flint Enterprises would make money hand-over-fist once they converted the building into a gambling casino. With obscure, recent laws allowing gambling in certain locations, Skin-Flint hadn't mentioned to its investors that historic buildings renovated with private moneys were eligible to become gambling establishments. That minor detail wouldn't block their path to rapid riches as managers of the soon-to-be renamed Humboldt Palace.

## Questions

1. What are Mr. Skinner and Mr. Flint saving?

2. Who else has helped Skin-Flint Enterprises in saving this building?

3. What does it appear Mr. Skinner and Mr. Flint are doing to their community and investors?

4. What does the investors' reaction to the Skin-Flint proposal tell about them?

5. Is the community aware of the entire plan that Mr. Skinner and Mr. Flint have for their business use of the hotel? If they were, do you think they would support that plan?

6. What do you think of Mr. Skinner's and Mr. Flint's plan?

# Deus Vult

## Topic

The Crusades

## Objective

Students will describe how Christians treated Jews after the initial call by the Pope for a holy crusade in 1095.

## Materials

- the accompanying vignette It Is God's Will (pages 76 and 77)

## Preparation

Make a copy of It Is God's Will for each student.

## Procedure

1. As you begin a unit on the Crusades, place students in cooperative teams and pass out the vignette.

2. Orally read It Is God's Will in class and have students answer each of the follow-up questions on their own.

3. Allow time for group discussion on the follow-up questions. After sufficient group discussion, have a whole class discussion about the conflict within the vignette.

4. Inform the class that while the characters within the story were fictitious, it accurately portrays the reactions of numerous European peasants to the call by Pope Urban II for a holy crusade. (See the Background section of this simulation.)

## Background

While Pope Urban II envisioned a holy crusade as an organized military campaign led by battle-tested nobility, the initial response surely came as a shock to him. Thousands of peasants in France and Germany, full of religious zeal and a desire to escape their limited opportunities, gathered in riotous mobs that moved eastward across the continent, plundering villages (Christian and non-Christian alike).

# Deus Vult *(cont.)*

## Background *(cont.)*

Viewing the non-Christian Jews as enemies and reasoning that the Pope had said to make war on the infidels, they began murderous assaults on their Jewish neighbors in the spring of 1096. The atrocities committed in Worms, Germany alone, left over one thousand Jews dead. It became so horrendous a debacle that local villages along the route of this "Peasant's Crusade" poisoned wells and ambushed the self-proclaimed religious mercenaries.

By the time they reached Constantinople, they were a ragtag outfit of outlaws. The Byzantium emperor gave them enough food and military supplies to get rid of them. Their numbers were ultimately decimated by the Turks.

"Deus Vult" was the Latin cry of these peasants, "It is the will of God." This activity is designed to demonstrate to students the horrors of misguided religious fervor. Throughout history, religion has often been a major source of conflict, perhaps running second only to economic issues. However, in an age where learning wasn't encouraged, most people couldn't read, and Bibles were extremely expensive and rare. These European peasants didn't have the Scriptures at their disposal to give them any real Christian guidelines. They simply interpreted the Church's stated wishes, "Kill the infidel."

## Extension

Students may do research on religious conflicts—past and present. In our own 13 colonies, religious intolerance could be found in places such as Massachusetts Bay Colony. In the nineteenth century, the Mormon Church met so much antagonism against its ideas that its followers trekked to a divine desert, which they named Utah. Of recent note, the conflict in Kosovo pitted ethnic Albanians, who followed Islam, against the Serbian Christian majority in Yugoslavia.

---

### Answers for page 77

1. Apparently upon the instructions of their Church, the farmer and others of his village were killing the Jewish population because they weren't Christians.

2. Answers will vary.

3. Yes. Answers will vary.

---

# It Is God's Will

Frederick thrust the sword into the little Jewish man. Impaled upon the sword, the man stared back at the exhausted Saxon farmer and let out a final gasp of air. Frederick had chased him through the streets of Worms for more than 10 minutes, his rage building around every turn. He had confronted the man at his shop and had given him a chance at life with a loud, simple, and blunt command, "Convert to Christ or die." Frederick now reasoned that he had no cause for guilt. It was the shopkeeper's own choice; he had run.

Frederick's act wasn't isolated. Throughout this Central European town, peasants were on a rampage against the local Jews. They were being sought out and slaughtered. The blond, husky farmer was tired and sat on an accommodating wooden bench outside a Jewish cobbler's shop. The owner lay slain inside. Frederick snickered, "He will no longer need the bench."

As he sat on the bench, he took stock of what he had personally accomplished on this spring day in 1096. Three adult males, two adult females, and four children (three boys and a girl) had fallen at his hand alone this day. He had also relieved his victims of a large amount of money. After all, he thought, it was fair compensation for this dirty, yet necessary, work for the Lord. The Church had called upon him and his neighbors for their help, and they had delivered. It was God's will, and He would be proud of Frederick. His bishop had told him so.

After an evening's rest, he would gather his belongings and join the others on the trek to the Holy Land. More plunder awaited him. There were more infidels to be killed. Perhaps he could get better land in Palestine. Even if he died in the process of eliminating these nonbelievers, he had the Pope's assurance that he would be forgiven of all sins. Anyway, he was content in doing God's will here on earth.

# It Is God's Will *(cont.)*

**Directions:** After reading "It Is God's Will," respond to the following questions:

1. What conflict is apparently going on in this story?  What appears to be the reason behind it?

_____

_____

_____

_____

_____

_____

_____

2. Do you think there are situations where religious zeal justifies killing others?  Why or why not?

_____

_____

_____

_____

_____

_____

3. Do people still persecute, or pick on, others for religious reasons today?  Explain.

_____

_____

_____

_____

_____

_____

# Crusade Bingo

## Topic
The Crusades

## Objective
Students will use maps depicting the routes of the various Crusades to employ latitude/longitude skills.

## Materials
- the accompanying maps of various Crusades (pages 82–85)—The First Crusade (1096–1099), The Third Crusade (1189–1192), The Crusades of Louis IX, Primary Crusader Routes (*optional*)
- the accompanying list of latitude/longitude coordinates (page 80)
- a resealable, plastic bag or envelope
- the accompanying Map Questions for Primary Crusade Routes on page 81 (*optional*)

## Preparation
1. Make copies of the various Crusades' maps (excluding Primary Crusade Routes) so that each student has a set.
2. Make one copy of the latitude/longitude coordinates, laminate it, and cut out each coordinate separately and laminate each.
3. Place the loose coordinates in a resealable bag or envelope for storage.
4. If desired, make a copy of Primary Crusade Routes map for each student, as well as its accompanying set of questions.

## Procedure
1. Group students in pairs. Introduce the activity by telling the class that today they will be playing Bingo. Explain that it will be a form of Bingo in which they will have to apply their knowledge of latitude/longitude with maps displaying routes of the various Crusades.
2. Distribute the maps to the students. Each student pair should have a set of three maps. While there are only three different maps, there are a combined total of seven different routes with latitude/longitude points on those three maps. Student pairs will either choose or be assigned one route of a specific European crusade. That route will function as a Bingo card.
3. The teacher randomly draws coordinates from the plastic bag, calling out the latitude/longitude measure.
4. All routes have seven oval points on them. To obtain "Bingo," student teams must have five points on their route called out by the teacher. In case of a tie, the team who has an identified point closest to Jerusalem will be considered the winner.

# Crusade Bingo (cont.)

## Background

From 1096 to 1270, there were eight major Crusades and a number of smaller, more fragmented efforts to regain the Holy Land for Christendom. The maps used in this activity highlight the Nobles' Crusades (The First Crusade) and the Kings' Crusades (The Third Crusade).

In 1097, the Nobles' Crusade brought about 30,000 zealous warriors from Europe into the Middle East. In Asia Minor, they initially defeated the Turks. However, moving south into Palestine, heat, hunger, and a lack of supplies relegated this crusade to 12,000 marauders who pillaged Jerusalem and killed Muslims, Jews, and Christians alike.

The Kings' Crusade of 1189 was led by Richard I (England), Philip II (France), and Frederick I (Germany). It fared no better than the First Crusade. Frederick died in Asia Minor, and most of his troops immediately went home. Philip and Richard continually argued over who would lead the Europeans, and Philip took his army and left after capturing a few Palestinian seaports. Richard was left by himself to deal with the Muslim leader Saladin. The best Richard could do was reach a truce with Saladin whereby Muslims and Christians could both visit respective shrines in the Holy Land in peace with the Muslims in control.

The Seventh Crusade, led by Louis IX of France, is included only to give the instructor another Bingo route to use in this activity. Like the previous excursions, it proved ineffective. It was unique in its approach, however. Louis decided to attack Muslim towns in Egypt in an attempt to draw forces away from the Holy Land. His last attempt, the Eighth Crusade, stretched that logic to the limit by invading Northern Africa, south of Sicily. There, Louis died of disease, and the Crusades died from a lack of further European interest.

---

### Answers for page 81

1. Marseilles, Genoa, Venice

2. to obtain needed supplies

3. Atlantic Ocean, Mediterranean Sea, Adriatic Sea, Aegean Sea

4. approximately 2,400 miles (*Hint:* Use a twist tie to plot the route and compare it to the map scale bar.)

5. Acre

6. the First Crusade

7. Spain

8. the Third Crusade

(*Note:* The Primary Crusade Routes map on page 85 has been included should the instructor wish to give students extra practice reading maps that deal with the Crusades.)

---

# Coordinates for Various Crusade Routes

## The First Crusade

| Robert of Flanders | Raymond of Toulouse | Godfrey of Bouillon |
|---|---|---|
| 51° N, 5° E | 44° N, 4° E | 48° N, 10° E |
| 49° N, 5° E | 46° N, 10° E | 47° N, 14° E |
| 44° N, 10° E | 45° N, 15° E | 44° N, 20° E |
| 41° N, 15° E | 42° N, 19° E | 43° N, 25° E |
| 41° N, 24° E* | 41° N, 24° E* | 41° N, 24° E* |
| 40° N, 30° E* | 40° N, 30° E* | 40° N, 30° E* |
| 37° N, 37° E* | 37° N, 37° E* | 37° N, 37° E* |

*Note:* The last three coordinates for all routes were the same as these nobles joined forces.

## The Third Crusade

| Richard I | Philip II | Frederick I |
|---|---|---|
| 50° N, 2° W | 46° N, 7° E | 48° N, 15° E |
| 37° N, 6° W | 43° N, 10° E | 46° N, 20° E |
| 40° N, 1° E | 40° N, 12° E | 44° N, 23° E |
| 43° N, 6° E | 37° N, 16° E | 40° N, 27° E |
| 40° N, 14° E | 36° N, 21° E | 38° N, 30° E |
| 37° N, 20° E | 35° N, 25° E | 38° N, 36° E |
| 36° N, 28° E | 35° N, 30° E | 36° N, 36° E |

## Louis IX's Seventh Crusade

| |
|---|
| 42° N, 5° E |
| 40° N, 7° E |
| 38° N, 10° E |
| 36° N, 15° E |
| 35° N, 22° E |
| 35° N, 30° E |
| 34° N, 33° E |

# Map Questions for
# Primary Crusade Routes

1. According to the Primary Crusade Routes map, what three southern European cities were apparently important stopping points for the Crusaders?

   _____  _____  _____

2. What might have been a reason for the importance of these cities?

   _____

   _____

   _____

   _____

   _____

   _____

3. Name four large bodies of water crossed by the Crusaders.

   _____  _____

   _____  _____

4. During the First Crusade, how far did the army coming from the Holy Roman Empire have to march to reach Jerusalem?

   _____

5. Name the Palestinian seaport that was the stopping point of the Third Crusade.

   _____

6. According to the map, which Crusade actually reached Jerusalem?

   _____

7. Which part of European land was already controlled by Muslims during the time of the Crusades?

   _____

8. Which Crusade totally bypassed Constantinople?

   _____

# The First Crusade (1096–1099)

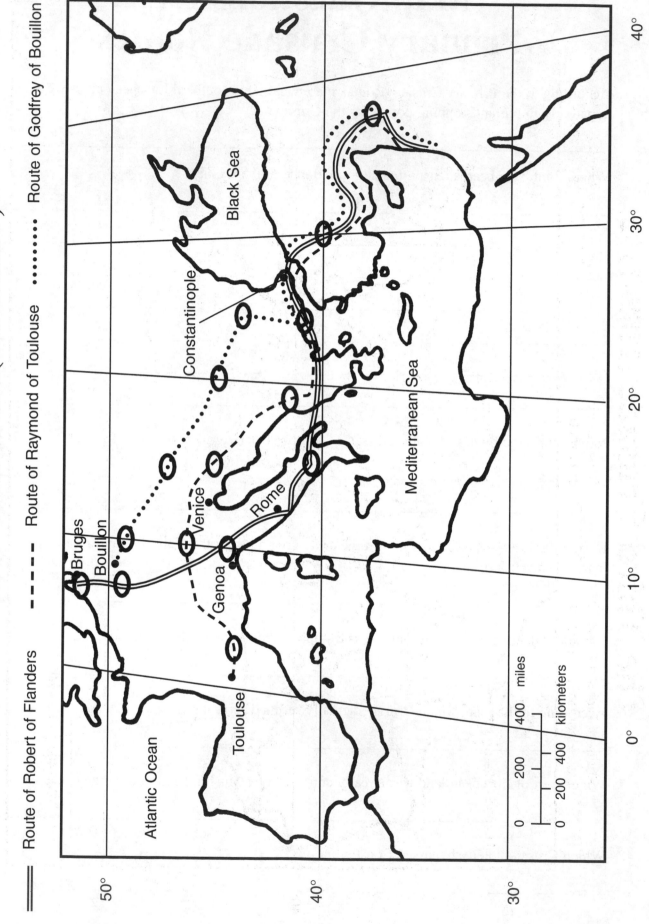

Route of Robert of Flanders

Route of Raymond of Toulouse

Route of Godfrey of Bouillon

Atlantic Ocean

Toulouse

Genoa

Venice

Rome

Bruges

Bouillon

Constantinople

Black Sea

Mediterranean Sea

0    200    400    miles

0    200    400    kilometers

50°

40°

30°

0°    10°    20°    30°    40°

# The Third Crusade (1189–1192)

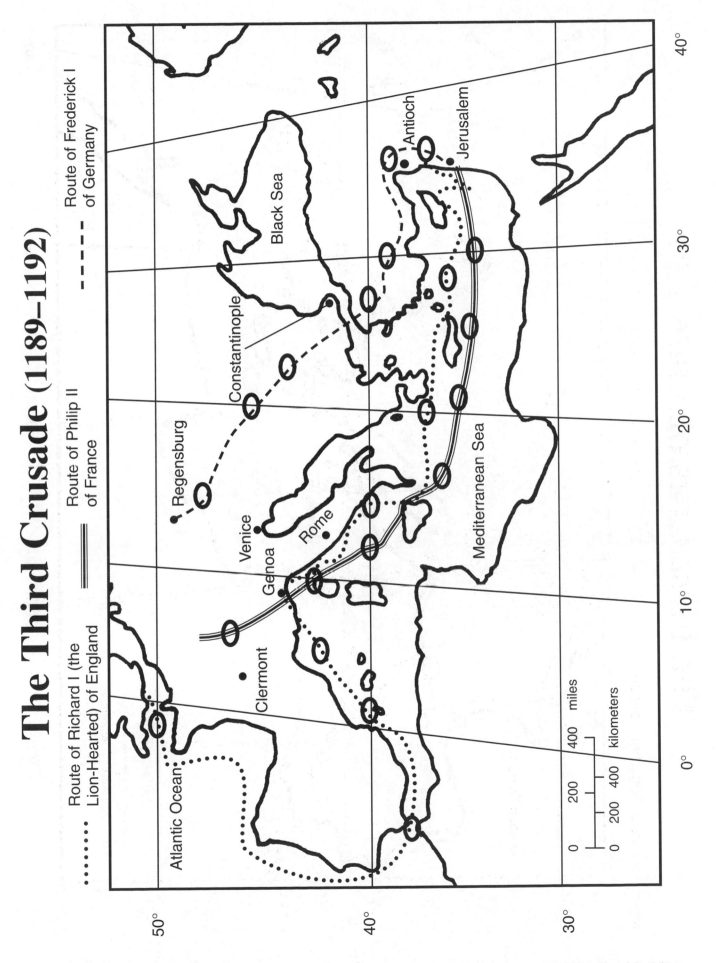

Route of Richard I (the
Lion-Hearted) of England

Route of Philip II
of France

Route of Frederick I
of Germany

Atlantic Ocean

Clermont

Regensburg

Venice

Genoa

Rome

Constantinople

Black Sea

Antioch

Jerusalem

Mediterranean Sea

0    200    400    miles

0    200    400    kilometers

0°          10°          20°          30°          40°

50°

40°

30°

# The Crusades of Louis IX

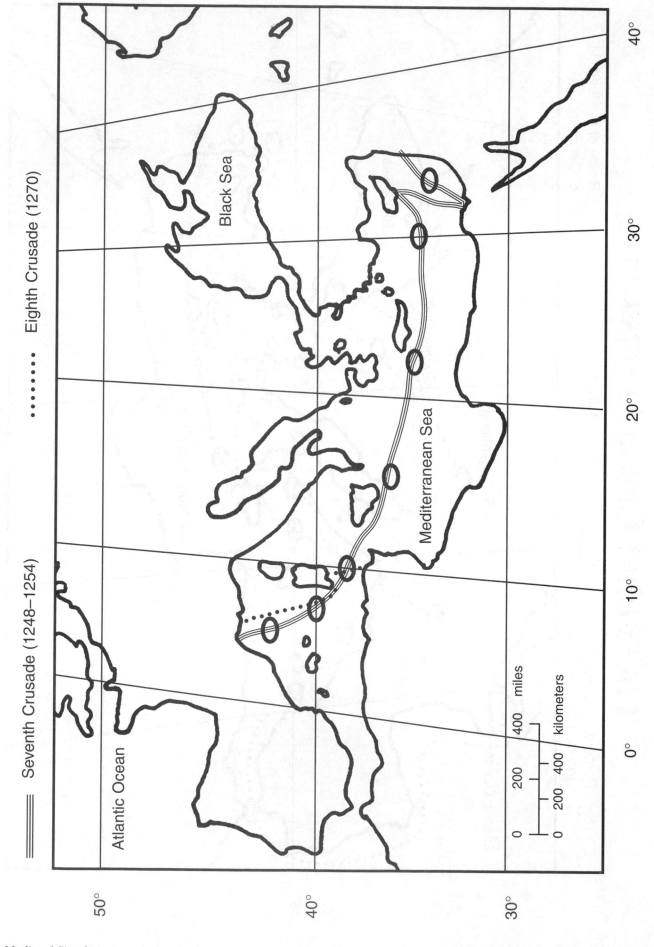

Seventh Crusade (1248–1254) ········· Eighth Crusade (1270)

Black Sea

Mediterranean Sea

Atlantic Ocean

miles
kilometers

# Primary Crusade Routes

**Land controlled by Muslims** (dark shading)

**Land controlled by Christians** (light shading)

**First Crusade (1096–1099)** — – – – – –

**Third Crusade (1189–1192)** — • • • • • • •

Atlantic Ocean

SPAIN

FRANCE

Clermont

Marseilles

Genoa

Venice

HOLY ROMAN EMPIRE

ITALY

Adriatic Sea

Mediterranean Sea

AFRICA

Constantinople

Black Sea

Aegean Sea

ASIA MINOR

Antioch

Acre

Jerusalem

PALESTINE

0°    10°    20°    30°    40°

30°    40°    50°

0    200    400    miles

0    200    400    kilometers

# The Great (Tasting) Charter

## Topic

The Magna Carta

## Objectives

1. Students will identify specific reasons for the imposition of the Magna Carta.

2. Students will explain that the main objective of the charter was to limit the king's power.

## Materials

- the accompanying set of role cards (page 90)

- a one-pound (450 g) bag of candy-coated chocolate pieces

- small paper cups or disposable bathroom cups (one per student)

- 10 plastic spoons

- 12" x 18" (30 cm x 46 cm) white tagboard (*optional*)

- gold spray paint (*optional*)

## Preparation

1. Make copies of the role cards so there will be one *King* card, three *Mercenary* cards, and one each of the *Noble, Knight, Merchant,* and *Peasant* cards for each cooperative learning team of four students.

2. Using a spoon, place 10 candies into each paper cup.

3. *Optional*: Cut out a crown pattern from the tagboard, staple the ends together, and spray-paint it gold.

## Procedure

1. With all students in cooperative learning teams of four, randomly select one team to fulfill the roles of the *King* and his *Mercenary* troops. To do this simply, have team leaders pick a number between one and 100. The team closest to your original number assumes these roles.

2. Have the king seated at the front of the room. (He may wear the optional gold crown.) The mercenary troops should dispense the cups with candy to each student, including the king and themselves. The teacher needs to admonish students to not touch the candy until the end of the activity or until they are otherwise instructed.

# The Great (Tasting) Charter *(cont.)*

## Procedure *(cont.)*

3. The teacher will randomly distribute a set of role cards to the remaining teams so that a *Noble, Knight, Merchant,* and *Peasant* are on each team.

4. Using spoons, the *Noble* in each team is to tax his subjects at the following rates:

   - *Knights*, who provide military service, pay him three candies.

   - *Merchants,* who represent the interests of townspeople, pay him four candies.

   - *Peasants,* who are almost totally subservient to the noble, pay seven candies.

   - The *Noble* should end up having 24 candies.

5. At this point, the *King* starts to order people around. He makes the following pronouncements:

   > "I, King John I of England, do hereby increase the scutage fee on all my nobles. Mercenaries, collect 14 candies from each noble."

   After *Mercenaries* have retrieved the allotted number from each noble, the *King* continues:

   > "I, King John I of England, do hereby order that all merchants pay me a tax of three candies. Mercenaries, collect my taxes."

   > "I, King John I of England, do hereby order that all knights loyal to their nobles pay me a tax of three candies. Mercenaries, collect my taxes."

   By now, the entire room, except the *King* and his *Mercenaries,* will probably be upset about losing their candy. *Merchants* and *Knights* will have had their candies reduced to three and four pieces respectively; *Nobles* will have had their fortunes shrink from 24 to 10 candies; and of course, *Peasants* will have only three candies. (*Nobles* could increase their taxes as well to recoup their losses.)

   Meanwhile, the *King* will seemingly be filthy rich. Assuming his *Mercenaries* were collecting from five other teams, the *King* should have 110 candies (14 *Noble* candies + 3 *Merchants* candies + 3 *Knights* candies = 20 x 5 (teams) = 100 candies + the original 10 = 110 candies).

   The *King* will announce:

   > "Now, I will generously pay my mercenaries for a job well done!"

# The Great (Tasting) Charter *(cont.)*

## Procedure *(cont.)*

6.  At this point, stop and discuss what is going on. (The *Mercenaries'* "payday" will be interrupted.)

    - Discuss the meanings of "scutage" and "mercenary." (See Background.)

    - How are the *Nobles* feeling? (*probably very upset*)

    - How about the *Merchants*? *Knights*? (*equally upset*)

    - Don't bother asking the *Peasants;* they don't count. However, do ask, "Which group is providing the most value to the kingdom in the form of food and labor?" (*peasants*)

    The *King* and *Nobles* had a basic distrust and dislike for each other. The King had to hire *Mercenaries* to do his fighting for him since *Nobles* wouldn't supply him with *Knights*. (See Background.)

7.  With the Magna Carta, the nobility forced the king to accept limited power. Have a group of *Nobles* read the following:

    "The King shall agree to reduce the fee of scutage. *Knights,* retrieve 10 candies for your lord (noble)."

    After the knights have taken such action, the *Nobles* continue:

    "So as to not interfere with the free flow of trade, unless in time of war, the *King* will return three candies to each merchant. *Knights*, collect three candies for each merchant."

8.  Once back in their teams, *Nobles* should return four candies to their *Knight* and two candies to their *Merchant*. Based on collections from five other teams, the *King* would end up with 45 candies. (After all, he is king, but with reduced powers.) *Nobles* would have 14 candies, while *Knights* and *Merchants* would have eight each. *Peasants* remain steady with three, and *Mercenaries* likewise remain constant with 10.

## Background

John I, the youngest son of Henry II of England, had inherited a significant kingdom that spanned the English Channel when his brother, Richard (I) the Lion-Hearted, died in 1199. It included England and lands in northwestern France. However, John was tyrannical and used various nefarious means, including extortion and murder, to try to consolidate his power. He alienated his nobility by increasing the tax known as scutage whereby nobles paid the king if they couldn't or wouldn't lend him military assistance in the form of their knights. They couldn't trust John to begin with, and that's why they didn't wish to help him.

John turned to mercenaries, soldiers hired for pay only, to enforce his taxes and orders. This further isolated him from his countrymen. To help pay for these personal tax collectors, merchants in cities began to feel the tax burden, and they were upset. Ultimately, John even was scorned by the most powerful social institution, the Church.

# The Great (Tasting) Charter *(cont.)*

## Background *(cont.)*

With the entire populace against him and French nobility seizing his own lands in France (the reason he came to be known as John Lack-land), John was forced to sign the Magna Carta in the meadow of Runnymede in 1215. There were over 60 provisions in the document, from allowing free landowners a trial by jury to eliminating trade restrictions except in times of war. However, the overriding effect of the Magna Carta was to delineate in a written article of law that the king himself had limited power and was not above the law.

Point out to students the fact that peasants, who made up the majority of the people in England, actually gained very little from the Magna Carta. Some repressive laws were relaxed, but in terms of actual power and money, nobles and rich merchants were the ones to make positive gains from the Magna Carta. Justice for the common man was still evolving and would take several hundred years more to come to fruition in England.

## Extension

Interested students may wish to research the Glorious Revolution of 1689 in which the first English Bill of Rights was created.

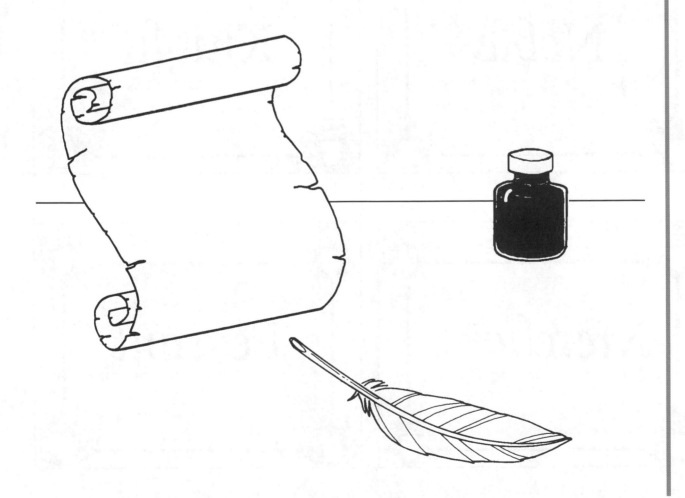

# Role Cards for the Great (Tasting) Charter

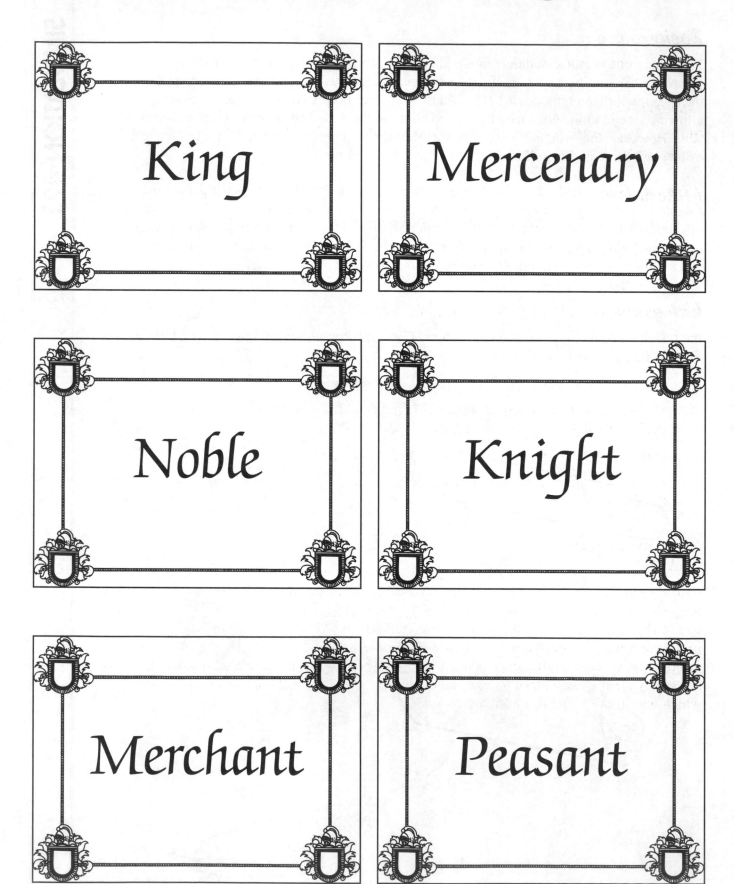

King

Mercenary

Noble

Knight

Merchant

Peasant

# Sunday Service

## Topic

Beginning of the Reformation

## Objective

Students will identify two weaknesses of the Roman Catholic Church that Martin Luther wanted to correct.

## Materials

- one copy of the situation Sunday Service (page 93) for each student

- overhead projector (*optional*)

## Preparation

Reproduce copies of Sunday Service dilemma for each student.

## Procedure

1. Divide the class into cooperative learning teams.

2. Use this activity as a way of introducing the beginning of the Reformation. Pass out the copies of the Sunday Service dilemma.

3. Have the class read through it silently while you read it aloud.

4. Allow the teams about three to five minutes to air the points of contention each has with the dilemma.

## For Discussion

Discuss the issues that the class has raised, listing them on the chalkboard or overhead. As a transition into the lesson, let the students know that at one point in time the scenario that was just discussed was quite frequently accurate when it came to Christian worship. During the end of the Middle Ages "indulgences" were methods of buying back sins or buying forgiveness for yourself, your family, or even people who had passed away. Before the printing press came on the scene about 1450, most people had no access to books of any kind since they were so expensive to have hand-copied. That especially applied to the Bible, which was usually kept in Latin or Greek.

# Sunday Service *(cont.)*

## Background

The power of the popes in the Roman Catholic Church grew with that of the kings. Bitter disputes arose between rulers of church and state. Church officials increased their part in political affairs more and more. When the popes returned to Rome, there were many disputes about the election of popes. This divided the church. Sometimes two or three men would claim the title of pope. These disputes hurt the influence of the church. The result was criticism of church affairs and of church teaching. The weakening of the religious unity of Western Europe led to the Protestant Reformation of the 1500s.

The movement began when Martin Luther, a German monk, protested. Martin Luther's posting of his 95 Theses was an example of a direct assault on the wealthiest and most powerful social institution within Europe during this time, the Roman Catholic Church. The Church with its ability to tax and crown rulers even had its own political entity, the Holy Roman Empire. In the early sixteenth century, Luther's threats on the church were met with charges of heresy and an eventual death sentence.

When the Holy Roman emperor sentenced Luther to something akin to internal banishment, German nobles rallied behind Luther providing him with safe refuge. These same nobles agreed to Luther's call to end indulgences and have the Bible available in German for all the people to read and interpret for themselves. They protested these and other aspects of the Church and so became known as "Protestants."

*Note to the teacher:* Some of your students may never have seen the inside of a church and are unaware of the difference between contemporary worship and that of five hundred years ago. However, most students will at least have an idea that something is definitely amiss in Sunday Service.

---

### Answers for page 93

1. Sample Answer: You have to buy forgiveness.
2. Answers will vary.

---

# Sunday Service Dilemma

It is Sunday morning. You are preparing to attend worship services at a local church. As you are about to enter the church, a church official greets your family with a collection plate and asks if you would like to buy some forgiveness this morning. Your parents place some money in the plate while you put in two quarters. You remember you had lied to your mother earlier in the week, and you want to buy back that indiscretion. (A quarter should do it.) You always buy a little forgiveness for dearly departed Uncle Harry who died two years ago. You figure Uncle Harry needs a lot of sins removed, so you usually buy back one or two each time you come to church.

Your family settles into a pew and prays silently. There will be another collection after the priest conducts a good part of the service in a foreign language that no one in your family understands.

The priest does finally address you in comprehendible language when he gives his hour-long sermon in which you get to hear bits and pieces of the Bible. You have heard that the Bible is the word of God, but at eight hundred dollars a copy, your family has not been able to afford one. Your parents have stated that there is no need for the expense of a Bible since the priest tells them exactly what to believe in it and interprets it for them.

As you are exiting the church, you place another quarter into the plate the church official is once again holding at the door as you leave. You really liked Uncle Harry.

## Questions:

1. What is "different" about this church?

2. Would you want to attend it? Why or Why not?

# One Smart Cookie

## Topic
The Black Plague/Medieval Medicine

## Objective
Students will identify the cause of and list ineffective medieval remedies for the Black Plague.

## Materials
- a set of teacher-created, review questions
- molasses cookies (one per student)
- overhead projector (*optional*)

## Preparation
1. Obtain the cookies.
2. Make a set of about five review questions over previously covered topics on the Middle Ages.
3. If the review questions are not in the student text, copies will have to be made, or they will have to be placed on the chalkboard or overhead.

## Procedure
1. As an introduction to a lesson on the Black Plague, instruct the class that you will have them answer several review questions to begin today's lesson. Furthermore, you have some startling news—"I've recently read in an education journal that small amounts of molasses apparently stimulate brain activity and help people, especially younger people whose bodies are still growing, to think more clearly and make better use of their memory. To that end, I am going to give each of you a molasses cookie to eat before you answer these review questions."

   (*Note:* Due to possible allergic reactions or taste preferences, students should not be forced to eat the cookies. Other items may be substituted.)

2. Have the students write out answers to the review questions.

3. When sufficient time has been allotted for students to finish, have them check their answers as each question is discussed.